1/28/2020

Dear Cameron -

It's been my pleasure to work along side you. Best to you in your future!

Sincerely - Marty Azola

THE AZOLA LEGACY ~ 50 YEARS

REBUILDING BALTIMORE

Martin P. Azola with Charles Belfoure

Publisher: Azola Building Services, LLC
4901 Springarden Drive
Baltimore, Maryland 21209

Printed in the United States of America.

Design: Dave Dobyski | davedobyski.com

Photography (majority of photographs): Anne Gummerson | annegummersonphoto.com

Copy Editing: Kaitlin Severini

Indexing: Beatrice Burton

Project Manager: Holly Ballard

Printing: Schmitz Press
37 Loveton Circle
Sparks, Maryland 21152
schmitzpress.net

ISBN: 978-0-692-14096-3

Library of Congress Control Number:
2018907047

The Azola Legacy ~ 50 Years Rebuilding Baltimore

Martin P. Azola with Charles Belfoure

Includes Index

DEDICATION

This book is dedicated to the loving memory of our son, Matthew.

Talented in so many ways, Mat was a proud and strong man with a generous heart.

Everyone he touched loved him. He will never be forgotten.

The Azola Family

CONTENTS

Left: William Patron and Charles Wagandt, developer, moving the George Ellicott House out of the flood zone.

FOREWORD

When you ask Baltimoreans to come up with a list of things that make our city great, make it different from other places and special to many of us, our historic buildings are always at the top of the list. Old buildings with their quirkiness and histories, their myriad of prior uses and possibilities for future new ones, are a core part of our identity. As we work to retain and attract new residents and businesses that increasingly value authenticity, our historic buildings are also a key to our future.

It takes a lot to preserve these special places. As the director of Baltimore Heritage, I spend hours every day advocating to save historic buildings and change policies to protect historic neighborhoods. Words alone, however, are not enough. We also need the hands-on doers, the people with the know-how and experience to look at a historic building, understand what's wrong, and know how to rehabilitate it properly. Luckily for us, we have three generations of the Azola family filling this role nicely.

This book, *The Azola Legacy – 50 Years Rebuilding Baltimore*, is a must read for anyone who cares about historic Baltimore. It's not only a primer on some of the most significant parts of our history, it peels back the curtain and gives an insight into the human side of brick, stone, and wood. In the chapter on Ruscombe Mansion, for example, we learn the story of Isaac Tyson and his chromium-fueled rise to wealth in the early 1800s while, at the same time, we step into the shoes of the Azola team as they carefully restore the building while fending off attacks from the resident black vulture. In the chapter on the Ivy Hotel, perhaps the most glamorous restoration project in the city, we simultaneously learn about the invention of the bottle cap (William Painter of Crown Cork and Seal Company was a prior owner) and relearn the value of having longstanding skilled artisans in Baltimore, as our own G. Krug and Son Ironworks dug through its 208-year-old files and found the original design of the metalwork that adorns the front facade so that the Azolas could replicate missing pieces exactly.

Above all, *Rebuilding Baltimore* reminds us that just as our great historic buildings were the work of the owners, architects, and craftsmen who dedicated themselves to the job, preserving and reusing them today doesn't just happen. This work, too, requires skill and dedication, and sometimes a little luck. I hope you enjoy stepping into the shoes of the Azola family as they share their experiences with Baltimore's iconic historic buildings and their wonderful work to keep them standing.

Johns Hopkins
Director, Baltimore Heritage, Inc.

PREFACE

Maybe we were just lucky, living here in Baltimore, having chosen the business of building preservation. From seventeenth-century log cabins to Civil War mansions to twentieth-century monuments, more than 80 percent of Maryland's historic buildings are in this fascinating town. The Azola family is fortunate to have been able to touch many of them over the past 50 years, and there are a number of interesting stories we feel compelled to share. We've chosen 26 conservation and rehab projects that span the history of Baltimore.

"Never get emotionally involved in real estate," my dad used to say. He was, of course, trying to teach fiscal discipline. But historic preservation is based on emotion to a large degree. Nothing beats that first experience of "the glow from within,"—that warm feeling engulfing you after your first glimpse of a finished project. The Azolas have been fortunate, indeed, to have felt the glow many times while also making a living. It doesn't get much better than that.

My dad, Joseph Azola, was a successful first-generation Italian-American contractor in Detroit during the 1940s and 50s, where he built roads, treatment plants, and bridges…big things. We moved around a lot to places like Chicago, Detroit, Phoenix, Chicago, Baghdad, Basra, and then Chicago again. In 1963, Dad announced that we were moving to this neat city near the Atlantic Ocean called Baltimore. His new job was to rebuild the area known as Joppatowne. And so, it began . . . the love for historical preservation, working in the town of Joppa, which was one of Colonial Maryland's six ports of entry, long predating the yet-to-come city of Baltimore.

I, personally, didn't set out to do preservation work. Being in the U.S. Air Force, I wanted to be a fighter pilot. But my wife, Lone, made it perfectly clear that if I continued in that direction, she would become a Pan Am stewardess. Message received, and I pursued civil engineering instead. The Alaskan air base we were assigned to was built by the Russians during World War II. My first job was to maintain the structures. Not terribly exciting, but so began my interest in buildings and their design, problems, and solutions. It was now 1973, and there were many building rehab opportunities all over Baltimore, so Lone and I came back and I joined my dad's business.

Building rehab, adaptive reuse, and true preservation boomed in the 1980s and all through the rest of the twentieth century. Our firstborn, Tony Azola, asked if he could come home and work with us in 2002, after he had participated in the rescue efforts of 9/11 as a member of the team that mapped the hot spots. And so started the third generation of family involvement. Tony is now corporate president for Azola Building Rehab, Inc.

Our second son, Matthew Azola, was a hands-on guy. He'd rather "swing a hammer than ride a desk," as he used to say. He worked with us for many years running projects in the field. We lost Mat in 2011, but he and his contributions to our efforts were extraordinarily significant, and so very memorable. He was everyone's hero.

The youngest member of our team, and our only daughter, Kirsten Azola, joined up after college graduation to parlay her talents in interior design. With a great eye for color, and more good taste than all the men combined, she contributed many of the beautiful finishing touches to our projects.

And then there is my wife of 50 years, Lone Azola. Thank goodness for Lone. Over all these years and hundreds of projects, Lone still keeps the books, manages the money, and has kept us all out of trouble . . . mostly. Don't let her pretty appearance and magnetic personality fool you. She was listening really well to my dad's advice about fiscal discipline.

Over the course of our work on Baltimore's legacy buildings, we have literally been attacked by vultures, buzzed by bats, and scared by snakes. We've found everything from Colonial coins to human skeletons, from player pianos to letters from wounded Civil War soldiers and bottles of fine cognac. It's been such an exciting and unique ride that we felt compelled to tell these true stories.

The Azola family hopes you enjoy reading *The Azola Legacy - 50 Years Rebuilding Baltimore*.

Marty Azola

ACKNOWLEDGMENTS

Holly Ballard is the genius behind the production of this book. She and her husband, John, have been family friends for more than 35 years, but until now, we have marveled at her talent from afar. Without Holly's organizational skills, this publication would have been done at the neighborhood copy center, in black and white, with a staple in the upper left-hand corner.

I would also like to acknowledge **Charles Belfoure**, a good friend and colleague who penned this fine manuscript after poring over thousands and thousands of documents. As an architect and a published author, he has brought to life the architectural challenges faced in the restorations, while portraying the uniqueness of each project.

And, to **Dave Dobyski**, thank you for all of the weekend meetings on the eastern shore, and for designing this exciting book. You will probably never want to look at another historical photo for many years to come, but your perseverance and determination to design this beautiful book is truly appreciated.

Anne Gummerson, our most talented photographer and friend since the 1980s, has done a spectacular job capturing the best images of the projects. Thank you ever so much for lending us your talent for so many years.

The advice of our bookseller, **Ed Berlin** of the Ivy Bookshop in Baltimore, has been very important to this effort, and we thank him profusely. It was Ed who suggested the logic of telling our story via a history of our town, the inclusion of lots of interesting photos, and the disclosure of our many surprising, and interesting, backstories. We are fortunate to have had access to such an experienced resource.

The huge task of copy editing has been admirably handled by **Kaitlin Severini,** and we thank her very much. **Beatrice Burton** was responsible for the indexing.

There is one other man who must be acknowledged. **John Felkner** of Union Bridge, Maryland, started work with us in 1985 restoring the Oregon General Store. Over the years he had a hand in the Stephen Cockey House, Taylor's Hall, the Old Baltimore County Jail, Pimlico (he personally made the finish-line marker), Solomon's Corner, the Barn at Windy Gates, the Ivy Hotel, and numerous others. John was our son Mat's friend too, and for that we are eternally grateful.

And, most important, here's a huge thanks to the many hundreds of good folks who actually did the work! Our corporate motto over these 50 years has been "you are only as good as your men and women in the field," and that sentiment is unquestionably true. We have indeed been blessed to have worked alongside the most talented and quality-conscious tradesmen in America. We salute you all.

Baltimore was an afterthought. Just a convenient place for a warehouse and a wharf to ship out farm goods for a local landowner, Charles Carroll of Annapolis and the Maryland Colony. Though officially created in 1729, it took many years for any buildings to be erected in Baltimore Town. The real interest lay in present-day Baltimore County, which once spanned from Cecil to Frederick Counties. It was there that Cecil, the Second Lord

1697-1860:
THE ASCENT OF TOWN & COUNTRY

Baltimore who owned the colony, had distributed land grants to men of means to farm and make the north part of his colony prosperous. With farms, mills, and mines, they did just that. These men were not absentee landlords but lived on their properties in large, though not fancy, homes, some of which still stand today as do some of their stone mills and villages. As these lands prospered, Baltimore Town grew slowly, with its own great houses for the land owners being built there, as well as an emerging streetscape lined with row houses. When an independent county separate from Baltimore Town was created in 1851, a new county seat at Towson Town was designated and with it came the need for government buildings. A community flourished in Towson with substantial houses, businesses, and churches. The north portion of Lord Baltimore's colony had become a resounding success.

Fate of local [...] determined at [...]

Continued from page 1.

had for a price for use at the Hotel site. The volun-

"teer comp[...] Cockeysvil[...] reactivated[...] The [...]

Taylor Hall in 1971. Originally built in Cockeysville in the early 18th century, it is to be reb[...]

Builder to preserve house by [...]

AZOLA, From D1

Genstar defended itself through losing battles before the Board of Appeals and at the Circuit Court level when Azola, a builder who specializes in restorations, stepped in. He agreed to dismantle the house and reassemble it for sale on land his company owns. Genstar agreed to pay the cost of moving the house

ley and Falls roads.

Azola discovered this to be the Stephen Cockey house, also built around 1725 and named for its owner between 1784 and 1797.

It was part of an early farm called "Poor Jamaica Man's Plague." Azola took over the demolition contract on it and dismantled the pieces, numbered them and

1776, but the bones turned o[...] pig bones instead.

Both Azola and Paul F. M[...] his project manager, are me[...] of the county's Landmarks C[...] sion, and John McGrain, exe[...] secretary of the commission[...] county planner, is pleased [...] historic old homes will rise [...] even if in new locations

TAYLOR'S HALL

In 1983, vandals set fire to the 1697 house at Padonia and York Roads in Cockeysville, a property that was owned by the Genstar Stone Products Company. Believing it too damaged to be repaired, Genstar wanted to demolish it. But the Baltimore County Landmarks Preservation Commission took them to court to block the demolition of the rare seventeenth-century house. In the midst of a legal battle, an unusual offer was brought to the table—to buy the house and move it to Rockland, a nineteenth-century mill village and National Register district at the corner of Old Court and Falls Roads. Genstar would pay for the move, and the Azola company would do a historically accurate reconstruction of the house at its own cost.

Taylor's Hall has an impressive history. Built in 1697 by Joseph Taylor, it was purchased between 1725 and 1727 by Thomas Cockey, one of the founders of Cockeysville in Baltimore County. When Cockey died in 1737, the house and 2,500 acres of surrounding land were inherited by his son, Thomas Cockey Deye. A prominent Maryland statesman, Deye served in the Maryland House of Delegates and was present as Speaker of the House when George Washington resigned his commission at the statehouse in Annapolis in 1783. Members of the Cockey family lived there until the mid-1800s, when it was sold to Richard Padian, after whom Padonia Road is named.

At the time, the practice of building additions to an original house was a uniquely American one. European homeowners almost never added on, largely because of the lack of adjacent land, or they would simply move to a bigger home rather than build. Taylor's Hall is a textbook example of the early American residential building process. The original house was quite modest, a one-and-a-half-story, gable-roof log structure with a large kitchen fireplace and sleeping loft. Log construction was a building technique brought to America not by English colonists, but by Swedes and Finns in their colonization of New Sweden in the Delaware region beginning around 1638. Log construction was quicker and cheaper

PROPERTY OVERVIEW

Property Name: Taylor's Hall

Original Address: Padonia Road, Cockeysville, Maryland

Current Address: Falls Road, Brooklandville, Maryland 21022

Date Built: 1697

Date Restored: 1987

Architectural Style: Vernacular, telescope

Original Architect: Unknown

Original Use: Residence of Joseph Taylor, Thomas Cockey, and Thomas Cockey Deye

Current Use: Private Residence

Developer: Martin P. Azola, Inc.

Contractor: Martin P. Azola, Inc.

Architect: Lawrence J. Link Jr.

Historic Designation: National Register of Historic Places, Baltimore County Landmark

Dismantling begins, 1986

The stone addition comes down, stone by stone.

than using English traditional methods, and it was passed on to Welsh settlers in Pennsylvania. Log construction was then spread across the American frontier by tens of thousands of settlers, until the easier wood balloon-framing technique replaced it in the 1850s. But log construction continued well into the late-nineteenth century in some sections of the country. Two types evolved. A log cabin is usually one or one-and-a-half stories and built with round logs, while a log house is two stories with hewn or squared logs.

As with most early American building additions, the Taylor's Hall additions were built in the telescope plan, with the next building, a two-story log structure, constructed deeper so that the original building could fit within its end. The first two buildings had hewn logs with dovetail corner notching, and chinking and daubing in the horizontal joints between the logs. A house with exposed logs was extremely rare in the eighteenth and nineteenth centuries; most were immediately clad with wood siding or stucco. Or, if the owner was too poor, they would whitewash the logs. It was after the hundredth anniversary of Lincoln's birth in 1909 that log houses in America had their cladding taken off. Each new addition to Taylor's Hall was larger and more expensive; the last was a handsome 30-foot-wide, two-story limestone structure with a portico entry. The stone building technique seen here in Baltimore County had migrated south with German settlers who had come from Pennsylvania.

The word "move" is misleading. It did not mean picking up and transporting the entire structure on a truck the five miles to Rockland. It meant disassembling the historic house

The log sections re-erected.

as if it were a giant jigsaw puzzle, numbering and photo-graphing each component, and then completely rebuilding the house from scratch. So, with great care, every piece of Taylor's Hall was documented as it was painstakingly dismantled and trucked to its new site in Rockland. Taking apart a historic house also means finding hidden treasures—including a staircase, covered-up windows, and a perfectly preserved wedding invitation addressed to the daughter of the owner, Richard Padian.

On closer examination, half of the 290-year-old logs were rotten or had been burned, and important cut stones for window heads and door openings were lost in the mountains of rubble delivered.

The hall's old roof structure didn't meet new building codes. But under the guidance of the Baltimore County Landmarks Preservation Commission and the Maryland Historical Trust, the house was rebuilt on a new founda-tion with a full basement. With great attention given to historic detail, stonemasons handpicked the limestone pieces and rebuilt the stone wall, and the original roof framing was used to re-create the roof profile with wood shingles. The original divided-lite windows, pine plank flooring, and log structures were restored and reinstalled. But architect Lawrence J. Link Jr. designed an entirely new house and built inside the old one using new parti-tions and new heating, air-conditioning, plumbing, and electrical systems. Once under way, it seemed to make

You never know what you can buy for a dollar.

That's all that was paid for one of Baltimore County's oldest surviving houses, Taylor's Hall. By reducing it to a pile of stone and wood then completely reconstructing it from the ground up, the house was saved. But the original $300,000 estimate of the restoration more than doubled before it was done.

sense to add a few additions, and the scope mushroomed. A new two-story rear wing containing a kitchen, family room, and master bedroom suite was also constructed as part of the rebuilding. A couple from Baltimore had heard of the project and became the reconstructed house's new owners. With DLF Design Associates of Timonium, Maryland, they selected an interior design scheme in keeping with the eighteenth- and nineteenth-century history of the house, making the project a complete historic rehabilitation both inside and out.

Left: Well-preserved wedding invitation found

STEPHEN COCKEY HOUSE

At the same time Taylor's Hall was being saved, a builder called and said he was demolishing an old house behind the Greenspring Inn to make room for the expansion of a shopping and office complex called Greenspring Station, and Azola could have the flooring he had salvaged. From a picture in *A History of the Greenspring Valley* by Dawn F. Thomas it was discovered that the house, which was built in 1725 on a tract of land called Poor Jamaica Man's Plague, had belonged to Stephen Cockey, who had lived there from 1784 to 1797. It was one of the original homesteads of the family who had founded Cockeysville, Maryland. So, to the delight of the Baltimore County Landmarks Preservation Commission, another rare house would be saved and moved by the Azola company.

The Cockey House would be relocated to a one-acre lot in the National Register district of Rockland Village at Falls and Old Court Roads and sit next to Taylor's Hall. It was another house typical of the early eighteenth-century building process, but was the chronological reverse of Taylor's Hall, with a one-and-a-half-story original stone structure with end chimneys and a sleeping loft built first, then a two-story log addition clad with wood clapboarding built next. Telescoped against the stone house, the log house was far grander in design, containing a center hall, a formal parlor, and a dining room, meaning the family had become more prosperous. But now, the homestead was in terrible condition, vacant and engulfed by vegetation.

The same dismantling process was used as was used on Taylor's Hall. The stones, timbers and logs, the fireplace, windows, and doors of the Cockey House were carefully numbered for accurate reconstruction on a new foundation. Even the building's orientation to compass direction was noted. And like Taylor's Hall, fascinating artifacts were found in its deconstruction—Ben Franklin–style eyeglasses, coins, bottles, a gun, a powder flask, and high-topped shoes. But the most interesting find was a cache of bones under the dining room floor, raising speculation that something evil had occurred in this house.

PROPERTY OVERVIEW

Property Name: Stephen Cockey House

Original Address: 10751 Falls Road, Towson, Maryland 21204

Current Address: Falls Road, Brooklandville, Maryland 21022

Date Built: 1725

Date Restored: 1988

Architectural Style: Vernacular

Original Architect: Unknown

Original Use: Residence of Stephen Cockey

Current Use: Private Residence

Developer: M. P. Azola, Inc.

Contractor: M. P. Azola, Inc.

Architect: Lawrence J. Link Jr.

Engineer: G. W. Stephens & Associates

Awards: Feature Performance Award—*Professional Builder Magazine*, 1989

Grand Award—Best in American Remodeling, *Professional Builder and Remodeler*, 1991

Stephen Cockey House, 1917

"These aren't human bones; they're pig's bones."

Given Stephen Cockey's father's violent reputation described by his mother, Prudence, three years after she left him, bones that were found during the renovation may have had a sinister story behind them. Thomas Cockey had reputedly whipped and stabbed a black servant; stabbed his son, John; and offered his favorite daughter, Achsah, 1,000 pounds to poison her mother. He had ordered Prudence out of the house at the point of a gun. But to everyone's disappointment, upon examining the bones, the Baltimore County coroner announced that they belonged to a pig, and everyone went back to work.

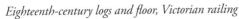

Eighteenth-century logs and floor, Victorian railing

Following the Secretary of Interior's Standards for Rehabilitation, the floor joists, roof rafters, and building stones were faithfully put back in place. While the log exterior remained hidden, its interior remained exposed, with the logs and chinking (a mixture of lime, cement, and sand) to keep the weather out. But although this was an extremely historic structure, the plan was for Lawrence J. Link Jr., the architect, to revise the interior to accommodate contemporary living demands. The challenge was to blend old and new. To replicate the original 24-inch-wall thickness, but also make room for modern insulation and wiring, 2-by-12 studs were framed, with a 12-inch veneer of original stone on the exterior. The fireplace was re-created with new brick and raised paneling representing the time period. The architect's design would make better use of the interior space by designing a rear addition with a garage and mudroom. The main idea was to not be able to distinguish the old from the new, so the design had to work seamlessly through the house over ten level changes. Building materials such as flooring, salvaged doors, and windows were reused, as was wood from Maryland barns for the ceilings.

Demolition of the interior finishes of the log portion prior to moving revealed that the original interior finish was whitewash, not plaster. Whitewash was a coating of lime and water, cheaper than white lead paint or plaster. The ceiling joists, which had been plastered, had decorative edges, indicating that they were also originally exposed.

The original poplar floorboards in the living room were 24 inches wide. Counting the annual growth rings revealed that the timbers they came from were at least 200 years old when felled in 1725.

Since the log portion of the house was covered with clapboard siding to protect it from the weather (unlike those in Taylor's Hall), they were in very good condition after 260 years.

At the corners of the log addition, each log was custom notched to fit into the joint. No two notches were alike, so it was important not to get them mixed up. Prior to dismantling the structure, each log in each wall was color-coded (blue for north, green for south, etc.), and each log was numbered down from the top. That system ensured that each log would be put back in exactly its original place in the assembly.

With a porch running the width of the house, its tall, first-floor, double-hung windows restored from a previous Victorian period renovation, and a new roof of wood shingles, one of the oldest houses in Baltimore County regained its architectural integrity in a new setting. Its long history will continue even though it turned out that it was never the scene of a murder.

Top: Stone living room, poplar flooring Right: Fireplace restoration

Before: Logs numbered for exact replacement order

After: Logs restored, chinked, and whitewashed

ROCKLAND GRIST MILL

Anthony Johnson was an original landed proprietor in the Greenspring Valley of Maryland, meaning he was one of the first Colonists to be granted land by Lord Baltimore, the absolute owner of Maryland. His son, Thomas, inherited his land and acquired more land in Baltimore County, consolidating it into one large farm, which became known as Rockland. When he died in 1791, Thomas's third son, Dr. Thomas Johnson, a practicing physician trained at the University of Pennsylvania, inherited this considerable estate. It was then augmented using income from large land holdings in Fells Point, Baltimore City, which belonged to his wife, Joanna.

Land that sits idle doesn't make money for its owner. But industrial development in Baltimore County in the early nineteenth century centered on the water power generated by the Jones Falls, where Rockland was located. The creation of the Falls Turnpike Road in 1806, which passed through the Johnson property, accelerated this development. Dr. Johnson arranged to have two miles of the new road built to connect his new business venture—a gristmill to grind flour—to the eight miles needed to reach bakers, retail grocers, and the expanding port in Baltimore City. He also had the authority to collect tolls from the turnpike.

From 1810 to 1813, using stone quarried nearby, Dr. Johnson built his mill in the vernacular, random-rubble form. It had three-foot-thick basement walls, with the upper floors diminishing to one-and-a-half feet in thickness to support a heavy timber floor and roof structure. He used the most modern technology of the day: the force of moving water to turn an eight-to-ten-foot-wide wooden wheel, which then turned a series of wood gears that ground grain between two huge millstones. Because it was such a specialized craft, a millwright was hired to design the millwork, and separate houses for the head and second millers were built on the mill's opposite corner of Falls and Old Court Roads. The mill was a sizable investment for the early nineteenth century, the 1820 census listing it as costing $25,000.

PROPERTY OVERVIEW

Property Name: Rockland Grist Mill

Address: 2201 Old Court Road, Brooklandville, Maryland 21022

Date Built: 1813

Date Restored: 1979

Architectural Style: Vernacular

Original Architect: Unknown

Original Use: Grist Mill

Current Use: Office Building

Developer: Rockland Mill Associates, LP

Contractor: J. R. Azola & Associates, Inc. & Martin P. Azola, Inc.

Architect: James R. Grieves & Associates

Engineer: George William Stephens, Jr. & Associates

Awards: Commendation, Society for the Preservation of Maryland Antiquities, 1979

Grand Award—Renaissance '83, National Association of Homebuilders, 1983

Historic Designation: Contributing Resource—Rockland National Register Historic District

Rockland Grist Mill, built circa 1813

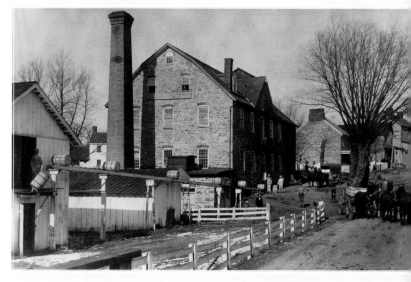

Dorothy Lamour worked at the Rockland Grist Mill.

In 1943, at the height of her fame, Dorothy Lamour, star of the Bob Hope and Bing Crosby "Road" movies, had married William Ross Howard III, descendent of the John Eager Howard dynasty of Baltimore, who had several country estates in Baltimore County. She moved to her husband's ancestral home and lived there until his death in 1978. In the 1950s, Lamour, whose career had begun to run its course, made the decision to become both a homemaker and the owner of her own cosmetics business, Dorothy Lamour Enterprises, which she ran out of the gristmill. A woman famous for her beautiful, unusual looks, she created her own brand of beauty facial cream and also a product called Jewel Gleam, which was used to clean jewelry. It was rumored that Dorothy Lamour herself helped to ladle her product into the cans. Her business closed in the 1960s.

Gristmills were built all over the Jones Falls valley, as they were a key industry, providing flour to the community. But despite its prime location on the Falls Road, which ensured market access, the Rockland Grist Mill did not do well financially from the beginning. The Napoleonic Wars that had disrupted agriculture in Europe were over and, with peace, the overseas demand for flour sank. In 1831 it was announced that the mill would be converted into a calico-printing business similar to the Rockland Bleach and Dye Works that had just opened to the south of the mill. In 1855, Dr. Johnson's son, William Fell Johnson, sold the mill. It burned down in 1857, was then rebuilt, and over the next 125 years, went through numerous uses, including becoming a gristmill again. After a failed attempt to use the building for artificial silk production, it was reacquired at public auction by the Johnson family in 1927. Of all the subsequent tenants in the mill, the most unusual was the actress Dorothy Lamour.

The mill was vacant in 1979, but when it was sold by the Johnson family to a developer, J. R. Azola & Associates, they discovered that it was filled with empty cans of Lamour's beauty products. The stone building, with its wood frame additions and missing waterwheel, was in forlorn condition. Turkey vultures had made a home in the attic. Floors were caving in, and windows were rotted out. In 1976, to give financial incentives to help preserve historic buildings, the IRS introduced the Federal Historic Preservation Tax Incentives Program (FHPTIP). If an owner was willing to keep the historic fabric of the building intact, upon completion of the reconstruction, they would get the credit. The gristmill followed the Secretary of Interior's Standards for Rehabilitation that the National Park Service had created in administering the new program.

In order to get the credit for the building, Azola had to keep the industrial character of the mill intact by exposing its interior heavy timber structure, fieldstone walls, and plank floors, and by restoring its 12-over-12 divided-lite wood windows and slate roof. The ramshackle Victorian-era additions were repaired and re-sided with wood shingles. The tall brick chimney was kept in place and repaired. Even the iron hoist bar to lower sacks of flour had to be preserved. A ten-foot-wide waterwheel was found in Virginia, cut in two, and then reassembled for the millrace. Before the wheel was installed, the millrace had to be excavated, as it had silted in over the years. Over 100 tons of soil was removed and dumped just south of the entrance road.

Top: Azola offices in the attic Right: Multiple additions

The mill became the headquarters for the Azola company; the rest of the space was rented out.

Dr. Johnson's mill, which had had bad luck from the beginning, now had a new life. Thirty-eight years later, one of the first mills in America to be preserved using the FHPTIP is still one of the most desirable business addresses in Baltimore County. People come to work not in a sterile office park, but in a totally unique building in an idyllic setting that reminds them of a quieter and more tranquil way of life.

ROCKLAND

THE FIRST INHABITANT OF THIS VILLAGE, DATING BACK TO 1706, WAS RICHARD GIST, FATHER OF THE REVOLUTIONARY WAR HERO, MORDECAI GIST. THE INDUSTRIAL DEVELOPMENT OF THE JONES FALLS VALLEY, MARKED BY THE BUILDING OF THE FALLS TURNPIKE ROAD, CIRCA 1806, AND LATER BY THE BALTIMORE AND SUSQUEHANNA RAILROAD, WAS THE REASON FOR THE CONSTRUCTION OF ROCKLAND VILLAGE, BUILT BY THE JOHNSON FAMILY TO HOUSE THE OWNERS OF AND WORKERS IN THE VILLAGE'S VARIOUS ENTERPRISES. THE VILLAGE ALSO INCLUDED A BLACKSMITH SHOP, FLOUR MILL, GENERAL STORE AND TAVERN. THROUGH THE HISTORY OF THE VILLAGE RUNS THE THREAD OF JOHNSON FAMILY INVOLVEMENT, INCLUDING THREE RESTORATIONS, CIRCA 1880, 1930 AND 1983.

★ ROCKLAND VILLAGE HOMEOWNERS ASSOCIATION, INC. ★
AND
MARYLAND HISTORICAL SOCIETY

ROCKLAND VILLAGE

After Dr. Thomas Johnson built the Rockland Grist Mill between 1810 and 1813, on the corner of Old Court Road and the Falls Turnpike Road, a village quickly grew up around it. This was a quite common occurrence all over rural Maryland in the late-eighteenth and early-nineteenth centuries. A mill was the economic engine of a community, whether it ground grain into flour or made clothes or rope. Housing for mill hands, the millers, general stores, blacksmith shops, and taverns sprang up beside mills, especially those located on a major road (like the Falls Turnpike Road). The entire village was usually a sole business venture by the owner of the mill, as it was for Dr. Johnson. The owner almost always built his home nearby his investment; the Johnson family built their Greek Revival home from 1836–1837, on a hilltop a thousand yards away.

A mill especially needs housing for its workers. Called the "Stone Row," a row of eight, four-story, gable-roof houses, constructed of local fieldstone, was built along the west side of Falls Road. The miller's house was constructed along with a general store, a tavern, a blacksmith's shop, and more small houses, totaling fifteen buildings. Some of them were log structures with clapboarding. Finding the dates when historic buildings were constructed is often elusive, but at Rockland, it is an easier task: the date 1813 is incised in stone on some of the buildings.

Despite its prime location along Falls Road and its use of water power from the Jones Falls, Rockland Grist Mill had financial difficulties from the beginning. It was then converted into a calico-printing works in 1831, but that business eventually failed as well. The Johnson family sold the properties in the 1850s but bought them back in 1927. In all that time, the adjacent stone buildings had been rented out as residences or businesses, but despite surrounding suburban development and the construction of a nearby interstate, the village and the mill both survived and became one of the very few examples in Maryland of an entire intact nineteenth-century mill community.

It was on a flight to his Harvard college reunion in 1980 when Robert H. Johnson, great-great-grandson of Thomas Johnson, who had grown up in Rockland Village, told his classmate, architect David Wright, how

PROPERTY OVERVIEW

Property Name: Rockland Village

Address: Corner of Falls & Old Court Roads, Brooklandville, Maryland 21022

Date Built: 1712–1880

Date Restored: 1983

Architectural Style: Vernacular

Original Architect: Unknown

Original Use: Housing, general store, chapel, blacksmith shop

Current Use: Residential

Developer: Rockland Village Partnership LP (Robert H. Johnson, David G. Wright, Martin P. Azola)

Contractor: M. P. Azola, Inc.

Architect: David G. Wright

Engineer: George William Stephens, Jr. & Associates

Awards: Grand Prize—Renaissance '83, National Association of Homebuilders, 1983

Historic Designation: Rockland Historic District, National Register of Historic Places and Baltimore County landmark

Bobby Johnson, Marty Azola, and David Wright, developers

Resident bats

Bats had infested the attics of Stone Row over the years, dropping mountainous piles of guano, which can cause serious, even life-threatening, illness to humans. The men who remediated the mess wore hazmat suits and respirators so they wouldn't become infected with histoplasmosis, a fungal infection of the lungs. Dozens of light bulbs were strung around the 150-foot-long attic, burning 24 hours a day. After weeks of endless light, the last of the huge bat colony flew away, never to return.

Stonework renovation

unique Rockland was and how he wanted to renovate his family's properties. The first step in accomplishing that, the two decided, was to convert the buildings from rentals to being owner occupied. Another critical decision was made on the plane—one group would do all the exterior renovations to insure historical accuracy. The village had been placed on the National Register of Historic Places in 1973, and retaining its architectural integrity was paramount. After the renovations, which included the installation of new utilities, the buildings would be sold individually as residences.

Most people buy one house at a time; very few buy 15 at once. But that's what had to be done in order to ensure the uniform architectural and historical quality of the exterior renovation of Rockland Village, which is what Johnson and Wright wanted. So, financing was arranged to buy 15 structures, and the renovations began. The houses would be sold individually, and the new owners could renovate the interiors as they wished.

Johnson and Wright formed the Rockland Village Partnership with Marty Azola, who had renovated the mill in 1979, and purchased fifteen buildings on fifteen acres. With meticulous care, the group followed the Secretary of Interior's Guidelines on Rehabilitation and did not compromise on quality. Mortar on the stone building was analyzed and replicated down to the chemical composition and tint, and divided-lite wood windows were restored or, if too damaged, replicated exactly. Even lighting fixtures for the restored porches were carefully chosen to be historically compatible. Over the 150 years of their existence, every roofing material imaginable was layered. Once all of it was removed, the original wood shingle roofs, which were re-created in Eastern white cedar shingles, were revealed. Some of the buildings were in such bad condition that they didn't meet life-safety requirements. In the six-unit Stone Row, the homes were not separated by masonry fire walls—the attic was wide-open for over 150 feet. Cinder-block fire separations were erected between each home to provide fireproofing.

Over the years, the exterior grade had been increased, such that the level of the dirt was higher than the interior floor. Water infiltration was a serious problem. To solve that, a perimeter underdrain system had to be installed around many of the buildings.

During excavation for plumbing in one home, the dirt began to smoke! Years ago, a large quantity of iron scrap

Left: Rehabbed, pre-Revolutionary War bedroom
Below: Modern kitchen addition

had been buried under the floor, which rusted (oxidized), creating subsoil heat. When the soil was disturbed and oxygen came in contact with the iron, the heat energy was released as "smoke."

Utilities such as water, sewer, gas, and electric were replaced in each house. Over the years, utilities had been snaked from house to house, rather than directly into each house from the main services in the street. Work was severely hampered because the adjacent road was a very busily traveled state road.

Falls Road has been widened several times over its history. While obtaining building permits, the developer was surprised to find that the road right-of-way was now located in the living rooms of all ten homes bordering the road. After asking the state to reduce the right-of-way, they said that if the homes were to be developed, they would have to be torn down, since the state owned the land inside the living rooms. After a protracted negotiation, it was agreed to reduce the right-of-way so as to just skirt the face of the roadside porches.

At that time, Rockland was the only National Register district restored all at once. During the rehabilitation, mortgage interest rates rose to double digits, but all the properties sold quickly. Although they were placed in private ownership, the sense of community and its historical integrity were totally preserved. The homeowners know this—and are proud that they live in such a special place. They don't live in the suburbs; they live in a village.

GEORGE ELLICOTT HOUSE

Ellicott City is a charming, nineteenth-century historic town in Howard County, Maryland. In 1830, it became the first terminus of the Baltimore & Ohio Railroad, the country's first railroad, and has the oldest surviving railroad station in America. But there's a curse on the town.

The town was founded by John, Joseph, and Andrew Ellicott, three Quaker brothers from Pennsylvania. In order to build a flour mill, the town was located at the confluence of the Patapsco River and a tributary, the Tiber River, making it prone to catastrophic flooding. Sixteen major floods have plagued Ellicott City since 1817, producing walls of water that swept through the town, wiping out buildings and killing scores of people. The worst flood was a result of Hurricane Agnes in 1972, which rose to 14.5 feet. That flood destroyed the house of Jonathan Ellicott, a descendant of the founders.

George Ellicott, Jonathan's brother, had built himself a solid, two-story house, a typical stone residence for its time, with a wood pediment front entry, a gable roof with two dormers and chimneys at both ends, and a center hall. Then, in 1975, Hurricane Eloise caused a flood with a nine-foot water level and ruined the house. The waters ripped through the 1789 fieldstone structure, taking out all the floors (including the second floor, where George, an astronomer, had his observatory), the interior partitions, and the finishes. Only part of the main staircase was spared. There the house sat in ruin until 1987, when preservationist Charles Wagandt organized an effort to stabilize the building and its addition (the mother-in-law's house) and move it to a safer location, from the south side of MD-144 to the north side.

The house also had a basement with windows, which was quite fortunate, as it allowed the professional house movers to easily thread a web of steel beams under the first-floor joists, then jack it up and set it on a trolley to be hitched to a Caterpillar tractor for the move. The George Ellicott House was gently placed on its new concrete block foundation across the road. The mother-in-law addition was just too fragile to be moved, so that building had to be

PROPERTY OVERVIEW

Property Name: George Ellicott House

Address: 24 Frederick Road, Ellicott City, Maryland 21043

Original Address: 27 Frederick Road, Ellicott City, Maryland 21043

Date Built: 1789

Date Restored: 1987

Architectural Style: Vernacular

Original Architect: Unknown

Original Use: Residence of George Ellicott

Current Use: Offices

Developer: Charles Wagandt

Architect: Jeffrey Lees

General Contractor: Azola & Associates, Inc.

Mover: William B. Patram, Inc.

Awards: Best In American Remodeling, Period Restoration—*Professional Builder and Remodeler*, 1991

Project of the Year, Award of Excellence—Home Builders Association of Maryland, 1991

Grand Award—Renaissance '91, *Remodeling Magazine*, 1992

Preservation Project Award—Maryland Historical Trust, 1993

Historic Designation: National Register of Historic Places

> *As the house inched along like a snail, people held their breaths, believing the house would crumble at any second.*

In April of 1987, with the George Ellicott house jacked 12 feet off the ground, it was ready to be moved the 100 feet to its new site. With its two-foot-thick walls of fieldstone held together by almost 200-year-old mortar joints made of just lime and sand, the building was towed at a snail's pace, similar to NASA's glacial towing of a missile. With a large crowd looking on and collectively holding their breaths, they watched as the house moved along, half expecting it to fall to bits as it shuddered while cresting train tracks. But the George Ellicott House stood firm.

completely dismantled stone by stone and timber by timber and then moved to the new site so the restoration could begin.

The new use for the Ellicott House would be for offices, but the historic structure was not strong enough to meet building code requirements for the heavier floor loads. A new steel framework had to be incorporated into the interior, with new wood-framed floors installed. The 1975 flood has devastated the interior, so all new historically accurate finishes had to be replicated. The wood window trim, plank flooring, stair railings, and panel doors were re-created. The interior of the two-foot-thick stone exterior was replastered. Under the guidance of architect Jeffrey Lees, interior partitions were set in their original locations, and detailing like chair rails, baseboards, and wainscoting was re-created. None of the original mantels survived the flood, but Mr. Lees was able to design new ones based on the style of the day, as well as the clear ghosting of the woodwork on the remaining fireplace plaster. The wood 12-over-12 lite windows also had to be re-created.

The mother-in-law addition had also been constructed of two-foot-thick stone, but in its reconstruction, a one-foot-thick stone veneer was applied to two-by-twelve walls to allow for insulation, wiring, and plumbing. The wood frame connector between the two buildings was also rebuilt, replacing a missing porch with a historically compatible modern one.

Besides the mother-in-law addition, there had been other wood-frame additions to the house that were not replaced. But the "ghost" of the additions, the outlines on the side of the house, were left to show their former locations.

When the restoration was finished, the house gleamed with the newly stained wood floors contrasting against the white walls with their detailing. Its new use as office space was completely compatible, as though one went to work in a beautiful home.

Unfortunately, torrential rains in 2016 and 2018 destroyed many buildings along Main Street, including the town's landmark clock. But the George Ellicott House stood high and dry.

Restored parlor

Kickoff set for restoration of 1789 Ellicott House

By Edward Gunts

Buoyed by a $100,000 gift from an anonymous donor, local preservationists are finally moving ahead with a $1 million project to restore the flood-damaged George Ellicott House in Ellicott City.

Historic Ellicott City, one of three non-profit preservation groups involved in the project, has set Saturday as the kickoff date for the restoration work, which is designed to

REAL ESTATE NOTES

turn the 1789 house into an office and retail complex. A ceremony will be held at 10 a.m. Saturday.

Built by a son of one of the founders of Ellicott City, the Federal-style house is the last of the 18th century residences that once lined the banks of the Patapsco River.

After being battered by floods in 1972 and 1975, the house was moved in 1987 to Frederick Road at Westchester Avenue in Ellicott City.

"As far as getting the basic job done, we're OK now," said Charles Wagandt, a builder and developer

See **NOTES**, 16L, Col. 4

The George Ellicott House in Ellicott City is to be converted into a retail and office complex.

GEORGE ELLICOTT HOUSE

Entry hall and restored stairwell

Ghosting of prior room, contemporary entry

Stairwell after flood

ROGERS MANSION AT THE MARYLAND ZOO

When Frederick Law Olmsted and Calvert Vaux won the design competition for Central Park in New York City in 1857, cities across America wanted their own version of the natural, picturesque public park. But Central Park was not the first city park in America; there were predecessors, including one in Baltimore. The first portion of present-day Patterson Park was donated in 1827 to Baltimore City by William Patterson, the father of Betsy Patterson Bonaparte, who had married Napoleon I's brother, Jérôme. The land had been part of his vast estate in the eastern section of the city. This gesture set a precedent for wealthy families to donate or sell lands for urban parks. In later years, other great estates of Baltimore became public parks—Johns Hopkins's summer home at Clifton and the home of Thomas de Kay's Crimea estate became Leakin Park. The Rogers estate would become Druid Hill Park, Baltimore's "Central Park."

PROPERTY OVERVIEW

Property Name: Rogers Mansion at the Maryland Zoo in Baltimore

Original Address: Druid Hill Park, Baltimore, Maryland 21217

Current Address: Mansion House Drive, Baltimore, Maryland 21217

Date Built: 1801

Date Restored: 2013

Architectural Style: Federal/Italianate

Mansion Architect: John H. B. Latrobe

Original Use: Residence of Lloyd Nicholas Rogers

Current Use: Maryland Zoo in Baltimore Offices and Event Venue

Developer: Maryland Zoo in Baltimore, Donald Hutchinson

Design/Builder: Azola Building Rehab, Inc.

Engineer: Skarda & Associates, Inc.

Historic Designation: Baltimore City Landmark

Porch addition and decoration, circa 1895

In Baltimore's early days, a few men like Patterson owned most of the land in the city. With so much land, men could either sell it for housing development or donate it for civic purposes. But first they lived on it, usually in a large house. The Rogers mansion of 1801, the present mansion at Druid Hill Park, was the third home the Rogers family had after two had burned down. Two wings of the mansion had never been completed as planned. The basement housed the kitchen and storage area. The first floor held the drawing room, salon, and dining room, which flanked a central hall. The second floor held five bedrooms.

In 1860, Lloyd Nicholas Rogers sold his 475-acre estate and house to the city. The property had already been well landscaped by the Rogers family in the English picturesque fashion, but Howard Daniel, the fourth-place finisher in the Central Park competition, was hired to design the park which included picnic grounds, lakes, and promenades. George A. Frederick, architect of the Baltimore City Hall, designed the pavilions that still stand in the park. The Baltimore Park Commission had the good sense to preserve the Rogers mansion and turn it into an administrative building. But the house was converted into a public pavilion in 1863 by John H. B. Latrobe, the son of Benjamin H. B. Latrobe, father of American architecture. He removed the original entrance, built a 20-foot-wide porch encircling the original stucco Federal-style house, and updated the interior in the Victorian fashion by incorporating Gothic arches, ornate plaster ceilings, and an elaborate stair that led to a new cupola.

The next renovation came in 1935, with an attempt to turn the house into a restaurant—"All Roads to the Mansion House," read an ad of the day. Billed as "every man's country club in the very heart of Baltimore," the restaurant, whose "air" was "cooled by nature," was not a success. In the 1940s the building was used as a day school for the Young Men's and Women's Hebrew Associations, then later housed the Maryland Zoo's administration office. The mansion was used more as an exhibit area in the 1950s, when the Hall of Jewels opened, showcasing exotic birds and small mammals on the mansion porch. The Hall of Jewels remained there for almost 30 years. In 1978, a $850,000 renovation under the direction of architect Michael F. Trostel modernized the mansion, and it was used for administration and education programing. The birds were relocated throughout the zoo. But by 2010 the mansion was again in a state of disrepair, and another renovation was begun by the Azola company.

The most conspicuous item of deterioration was the three-ton cupola that was leaning substantially. Its wooden structural members had rotted as the result of water infiltration, and structural collapse was imminent; workers in the offices below had to evacuate. New steel beams had to be installed, but the only way to get them up into the cupola was to design the steel in sections, which four men would then need to carry up the stairs that Latrobe had designed.

The porch had also sagged significantly because of water infiltration caused by broken drainpipes leaking into the soil beneath the supporting columns. Each column had to be jacked up to the correct height, then scabbed with new timbers below that had been connected with epoxy and bolts. As a result of the repair, the siding, windows, and interior wainscoting were now also level. The entire building had major paint and wood deterioration, so years of paint layers and temporary patching had to be removed for repainting. Latrobe's porch was never designed to support the heavy loads that it was used for over the years, such as parties, dinners, and dances, so some joists had to be replaced or reinforced. Windows too deteriorated to be repaired had to be replaced in kind in order to match the original units. New exterior storm windows were added and interior woodwork underwent substantial restoration, plus spandrel panels between windows were insulated. A state-of-the-art variable Freon heating and air-conditioning system was installed, as well as new carpeting and lighting. All three floors of office space were renovated, including a new office space that was designed under the broad perimeter porch.

Today, Rogers Mansion is an administration building for the Maryland Zoo in Baltimore and overlooks Druid Hill Park from its hilltop site. Thankfully, no one in Baltimore has to walk between graves to enjoy nature within the city.

Original mansion house, circa 1801

Shall we take in some air at the cemetery?

In the early nineteenth century, if one wanted to stroll on a paved path, go on a picnic, or admire views of the countryside, they had to go to a cemetery. Public parks did not exist, so tens of thousands of Americans yearning for open space visited cemeteries annually. Mount Auburn of 1831 in Boston was the first American rural cemetery, followed by Laurel Hill in Philadelphia, and, most famous, the 178-acre Green-Wood in Brooklyn, New York. Their designers, the predecessors of today's landscape architects, incorporated hills, woods, winding paths, lakes, and scenic vistas. By the mid-nineteenth century, the great popularity of cemeteries as "pleasure grounds" ignited a demand for the large public parks we enjoy today.

OREGON GENERAL STORE

General stores once provided all of America's dry goods; they were the mainstays of every community and town. If they served the employees of a particular industry, general stores were called company stores. An iron-mining town grew up in Baltimore County that was first called Ashland Iron Company Town and was later renamed Oregon Company Town. The Oregon General Store operated as its company store and post office, at the corner of Shawan and Beaver Dam Roads. It served mine workers and their families who lived nearby in 20 houses on Oregon land. Old store ledgers show the names of customers and the list of items often sold on credit if customers were hard up.

Oregon, Maryland, was named after the state of Oregon. This wasn't unusual; lots of towns all over the United States were named after states. Besides the one in Maryland, there were eight more towns called Oregon, which was the favorite of all the state names for towns, outranking Texas (including one in Baltimore County) with eight towns and California with seven. There was an Indiana, Pennsylvania, where the actor Jimmy Stewart was born.

By 1885, iron-ore mining had played out and all operations ceased in Oregon. Then local businessman Thomas Kurtz bought the property in 1892. After his death in 1895, his wife, Catherine, and their two sons operated the store until the 1930s. In 1969, Baltimore County purchased a little over 1,000 acres to create Oregon Ridge Park. And on that land sat the vacant Oregon General Store, dilapidated and decaying.

Baltimore County did not have the funds to restore the endangered general store and, because it was now on public land, it couldn't be sold or subdivided. But in 1985, Martin Azola devised Baltimore County's first public/private partnership, featuring a long-term lease of the property, private restoration funding, and the use of federal historic tax credits as part of the financing package. A new county councilman, Dutch Ruppersberger, became a champion of the project, and it continued when he became congressman of Maryland's Second Congressional

PROPERTY OVERVIEW

Property Name: Oregon General Store (aka Kurtz Store)

Address: Corner Beaver Dam and Shawan Roads, Cockeysville, Maryland 21030

Date Built: circa 1840

Date Restored: 1985

Architectural Style: Vernacular

Original Architect: Unknown

Original Use: General Store and Post Office

Land Owner: Baltimore County Department of Recreation and Parks

Owner's Representative: C. A. Dutch Ruppersberger (now Congressman)

Developer: Oregon General Store LP (Azola Family)

Contractor: M. P. Azola & Associates, Inc.

Architect: Baukhages & Associates (Jeff Penza)

Engineer: Skarda & Associates, Inc.

Land Planner: Daft, McCune & Walker

Awards: Builder's Choice Award—Commercial Renovation, National Association of Homebuilders, 1986

Achievement Award—Creative Renovation, *Professional Builder*, 1987

Historic Designation: Baltimore County Landmark, National Register of Historic Places

In danger of collapse, 1984

District. Over $500,000 in improvements were made without using a penny of public money. The county entered into a 50-year lease agreement, and the property was put on the tax rolls.

The 7,000-square-foot Oregon General Store was in bad shape, with some foundation problems caused by heavy rains. It had deteriorated and was missing windows and the porch was falling down, but was definitely salvageable. Many people wonder why a building would be built just a few feet from a busy road, but in the 1840s, there were no cars whizzing by—just the slow clip-clop of horses passing. But for its reuse, a decision was made to reorient the entry away from Shawan Road to the rear of the building, with a path from the parking lot leading over a little wooden bridge to an entrance court flanked by trees. Two sets of steps led to the lower retail level and the first level.

Severe water damage

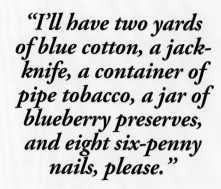

"I'll have two yards of blue cotton, a jack-knife, a container of pipe tobacco, a jar of blueberry preserves, and eight six-penny nails, please."

Today consumers can stroll down the aisles in supermarkets or discount and department stores and pick and choose the items they want off shelves and racks. But for most of America's history, there was no such thing as self-service shopping. Shopping meant walking into a general store, asking the clerk behind the counter for such varied items as canned vegetables, a hammer, cloth, paint, and candy, which he would then fetch and put on the counter to tote up the cost. Piggly Wiggly changed all that in 1916, when it opened the first all-self-service grocery in Memphis, Tennessee.

The original stair to the second floor still stood, and walls were removed on that level to create a more commercially viable space. To use the attic, a mezzanine was created by removing flooring while keeping some of the wood-joist floor structure in place. The stone walls of the building were cleaned of whitewash and repainted, the six-over-six wood windows were restored or replaced, and a new standing-seam red roof was installed on the main roof and on the porch roof, which extended across the width of the building. The wood frame additions to the store were also retained and restored. The architect was Baukhages & Associates.

Because of a prohibition on bringing public utilities west of Interstate 83, which would have set a precedent for large-scale housing development on adjacent farm fields, the store's sewage had to be pumped a half mile away to be disposed of. A well also had to be drilled for potable water.

When the project was completed in 1986, part of the first-level interior was re-created as a general store. The original counters contained a scale and cast-iron cash register with shelving and built-in drawers behind. Merchandise such as baskets and feather dusters hung from the stained beadboard ceiling. Paint analysis had revealed a delicate red pinstripe that originally decorated the blue walls of the store itself, and this was also re-created. The new store became Hayfields, a gift shop selling hand-made items such as toys, quilts, candles, and pottery.

The success of the Oregon General Store prompted Baltimore County to establish a program to recycle surplus properties, especially historically significant buildings. Today you can't buy a feather duster there anymore, but you can get a great steak. Since 1992, the store has been home to the Oregon Grille, one of the county's most popular restaurants.

Left: Oregon Ridge Park offered downhill skiing in the mid-1960s.
Right: Early Kurtz Bros. store marketing piece

OLD BALTIMORE COUNTY JAIL

When Baltimore County separated from Baltimore City in 1851, its new county seat in Towson now needed its own courthouse and with it, a jail. For a price of five dollars, Dr. Grafton M. Bosley deeded a five-acre tract on the west side of York Turnpike for the new buildings, and the Baltimore architecture firm of Dixon, Balbirnie & Dixon was hired. While their courthouse was designed in the Greek Revival style, their jail was done in the au courant Italianate. With the publication of *The Architecture of Country Houses* by Andrew Jackson Downing, which showcased the villa architecture of Tuscany, the style had taken America by storm. Houses, railroad stations, banks, and even jails used the signature square main building with a three-story tower topped by a low-hipped roof. But because it housed the undesirables of Baltimore County, it eschewed the usual fancy embellishments of the Italianate, like eave brackets and window hoods, but it used thick-coursed fieldstone walls to give a sense of strength and security.

Not only was its exterior up-to-date, so was its interior. No longer dank, windowless dungeons housing scores of felons, prisons by the mid-nineteenth century were designed humanely. The new Baltimore County Jail had the latest, well-ventilated, back-to-back, seven-by-twelve-foot cells (eight to a floor), with each housing one prisoner. The cells even had natural light coming in from eight skylights. Prison architecture of this period always included a domestic arrangement for the warden and his family, who would live in the front two-story section. The cellblock directly attached to the rear could be accessed by a single riveted iron-strap door. The warden conducted the administration of the jail in a front room on the first floor. The jail was completed in 1855 and occupied by its first warden, Sheriff Samuel P. Storm.

But when Baltimore County officials made an annual inspection in 1857, they complained about overcrowding and the fact that 12 of the cells had wood instead of iron doors. Instead of a slop bucket, the architects had provided

PROPERTY OVERVIEW

Property Name: Old Baltimore County Jail

Address: 222 Courthouse Court, Towson, Maryland 21204

Date Built: 1854

Date Restored: 2011

Architectural Style: Italianate

Original Architect: Dixon, Balbirnie & Dixon

Original Use: Baltimore County Jail and Warden's House

Land Owner: Baltimore County Department of Recreation and Parks

Owner's Representative: Barry Williams

Current Use: Offices

Developer: Towson Jail Associates, LLC (Azola family)

Contractor: Azola & Associates, Inc.

Architect: Marks Thomas Architects

Engineer: Skarda & Associates, Inc.

Awards: Award of Excellence, Historic Renovation, Home Builders Association of Maryland, 2011

The Wavemaker Award—Urban Land Institute, 2011

Preservation Award for Preservation Partnerships, Maryland Historical Trust, 2011

Historic Designation: Baltimore County Landmark, National Register of Historic Places

Cell block, 1905

The warden's office

New office in former warden's home

one toilet per cell, to be flushed once a day, but the officials complained of the smell, saying the water supply to flush them was inadequate. Reform was now an established goal adopted by prisons, and by 1858 the jail had a prison library and held Sunday church services.

The first escape attempt came in 1859, by John O. Little, who was serving time for manslaughter. He cut a hole in the wall of his cell and made a rope of bedclothes to shinny down, but he was caught immediately. Convicts facing longer sentences were transferred to the state penitentiary in Jessup. Most of the prisoners in the Baltimore County lockup were confined for months for petty offenses, especially vagrancy. Many inmates got themselves arrested on purpose in order to "winter" in the jail. Very infrequently, prisoners were held to await execution. A temporary gallows would be erected in the rear yard, and the hanging was not open to the public, the date and time of execution kept secret. Only one lynching was recorded when, in 1885, a black prisoner named Howard Cooper was dragged out by a mob and hanged from a tree on jail property.

In the following decades, the government always complained about the jail, so it was constantly being upgraded. But in 1905 the entire cellblock was completely taken down and rebuilt with 34 cells, corridors allowing light and air, and concrete floors and walls. The warden's quarters in all these years were barely touched.

As Baltimore County grew, so did its crime rate, and in 1956 a new jail was built behind the old one. Then, in 1982, another new jail was built on Kenilworth Drive. The original one was used for a work-release program until yet another new jail was built in 2006. When it was discovered that the vacant building, which was a local landmark, needed $700,000 for stabilization, an offer was made to the county to save the jail using the same public/private partnership the Azolas used with the Oregon General Store. The county agreed to a 100-year lease, and for one dollar a year in rent, plus taxes, the $1.7 million adaptive reuse was under way. The jail was also listed on the National Register of Historic Places, which made it eligible for federal and state historic tax credits to do a conversion to office space.

The warden's residence in the front, with its high, spacious rooms surrounding the two-story, sky-lit stair hall and its handsome curving wood stair, was a relatively easy space to rehab, despite large holes in the oak floors and chunks of plaster falling off the walls. It was the cellblock that was the challenge. In order to get the historic tax credit from the National Park Service, most of the cells, including their doors and surrounding corridors, had to be retained in the new design. This also included the bars covering the windows and the iron plate-bar doors between the residence and the cellblock. The cell walls had to stay because they were also load-bearing walls that supported the concrete slab floors of 1905. A compromise was reached: one floor of cells would remain untouched, and the others could be reworked for offices, kitchenettes, and restrooms, with the proviso that the original sliding steel doors could be seen from the corridors. Using jackhammers to remove 20 tons of concrete, new door openings were created and some cell walls were removed.

Upon completion in 2011, the project leased up immediately and has stayed near 100 percent since, attracting tenants (including many attorneys) who want to work in a rare historic space that has been so imaginatively adapted for a new use. Some people don't mind spending part of their life behind bars.

A former occupant of Suite G attempted to assassinate a presidential candidate.

A county jail is typically used as a temporary lockup for people awaiting trial or sentencing and who are then transferred to the state or a federal penitentiary. The Old Baltimore County Jail's most famous resident was Arthur Bremer, who attempted to assassinate presidential candidate Governor George Wallace in Laurel, Maryland, in 1972. He stayed in the jail before he stood trial. Sentenced to 63 years, he served his time in the Hagerstown state prison until he was released in 2007.

Before and after renovations to original stairway, circa 1854

TRINITY EPISCOPAL CHURCH

Two hundred years ago, getting a church commission was one of the most prestigious projects an architect could hope to receive because of the importance that the role of religion had in American life at that time. Whether fancy or plain, the design of churches reflected the religious values and beliefs of the particular society it served. They were often the most dominant architectural features of the towns and countryside in which they stood. A church spire would be the tallest structure for miles around. Today the importance of church architecture has become comparatively less important than secular building.

In the mid-nineteenth century, one architect in particular, N. G. Starkweather, designed many churches with great results. He received his architectural training as a builder in the 1840s. No architecture schools existed in the nation until 1865, so this was the way men learned the craft of building and design. Starkweather based his practice in Philadelphia and came to Baltimore in 1854 to design the First & Franklin Presbyterian Church on Park Avenue and Madison Street. The church, with its 273-foot, wrought-iron-and-brick spire, was the equivalent of a skyscraper towering over the Baltimore streets, an engineering tour de force for the period. It was also notable for its structural iron-roof truss system. With the trusses spanning from outer wall to outer wall, the need for thick stone columns that blocked the view of the worship space was eliminated.

Starkweather gave Edmund G. Lind, an immigrant from England, his first job supervising the construction of the church. Lind would become an important architect in Baltimore and throughout the South, his masterwork being the Peabody Institute on Mt. Vernon Place. Once an architect got a major church under his belt, he was in demand, and new church commissions would start to come in. One of these was a brand-new church in Towson, which, in 1854, had recently become the seat of government after Baltimore County had separated from Baltimore City. A new courthouse and jail were going up in the middle of Towson. Just a block away, a site was donated for Trinity Episcopal Church. Unlike most Episcopal churches, which

are founded by an Episcopal diocese, this one was started by a group of prominent citizens. The founders—the Ridgely, Taylor, Stevenson, Turnbull, and Smedley families—were all major landowners in the region.

A church architect would never repeat a design but would instead give his client something new in another style suited for that particular congregation. The Episcopal church tended to favor the Gothic form, which was the preeminent European Christian form, but also experimented with the Romanesque. So for Trinity Church, Starkweather chose the Romanesque, noted for its use of round-arch windows and doorways. The church would be cruciform in plan, with an arched truss ceiling running the length of the nave and 101 pews. The stone for its limestone exterior was donated by parish member John Ridgely from his nearby Hampton estate.

Because of the high cost and often complex design, church construction in the nineteenth century was a long, drawn-out process. When a church was dedicated, most of the time parts of the building were missing, to be completed when there was more money in the church coffers. This was true of America's biggest cathedrals, including St. Patrick's in New York City, which opened without its signature spires.

When Trinity Church was dedicated in 1860, it lacked its spire, vestibule, and transepts. In 1870 Lind added the spire and vestibule, and in 1892, when Baltimore architects J. Appleton Wilson and William T. Wilson added the transepts, construction was finally complete. A rectory and meeting hall had also been added to the complex. The interior was redecorated in the 1890s to include stained-glass windows depicting biblical scenes designed by Tiffany Studios New York. The chancel would be extended in 1926 by architect Laurence Hall Fowler.

As with most things, churches get old and begin to fall apart. After 130 years, the architectural firm of Schamu, Machowski, Doo & Associates was called in to design the restoration of Trinity Church. The architects had strongly recommended to the church that a builder should be brought on board early in the project, but Trinity wanted to pursue the traditional bidding process. The bids came in 50 percent over budget. The low bidder, the Azola company, suggested a structural redesign that wouldn't compromise the church's historical integrity and would bring the cost closer to the budget.

The biggest problem was the sanctuary floor structure, which was basically rotted out because of moisture seepage where the joists notched into the stone walls. To compound the problem, the ceiling had to be repaired from tall scaffolding, but this couldn't be done until the floor was fixed. The initial plan was to remove the historic floor, fill the basement with stone, pour a new concrete slab, and install a new wood floor over that. Then scaffolding could be installed to work on the ceiling and trusses. Nine months would have been required to sequence these tasks.

The builder's suggestion was to shore the floor structure from below, install the scaffolding above, and work on both tasks simultaneously. Rotten joist ends would be cut off and the old joist pockets would then be cleaned out and hung from a continuous new structural steel plate installed in a pocket on the inside of the stone walls. The steel would be hidden from view behind new wainscoting. In the 1950s the original stenciled ceilings had been painted green then covered with acoustical tile. The tile was covered with drywall to preserve the ceiling for a complete restoration when the church had the funds to do it. The historic floor was saved, and all other work was finished in accordance with the architect's plan, including restoration of the pews and a new HVAC system. The chancel was repainted a beautiful blue.

The results, all done in five months and on the original budget, garnered an award for both the architect and the contractor from the Baltimore County Landmarks Preservation Commission.

The angels' golden halos seemed to glow.

Each of the painted angels over the reredos, the ornamental screen behind the altar, was crowned with a golden halo. But subdued lighting in the sanctuary cast them all in shadow. To remedy this, Philadelphia lighting designer Luke Tigue was commissioned to create an entirely new lighting scheme for the church. He specified high-intensity spotlights that focused on each of the angels' halos, along with floodlights hidden in the roof trusses to show off its new paint job, blue with red accents.

Historic floor structure

Cherry wood trim

New wainscot meets old

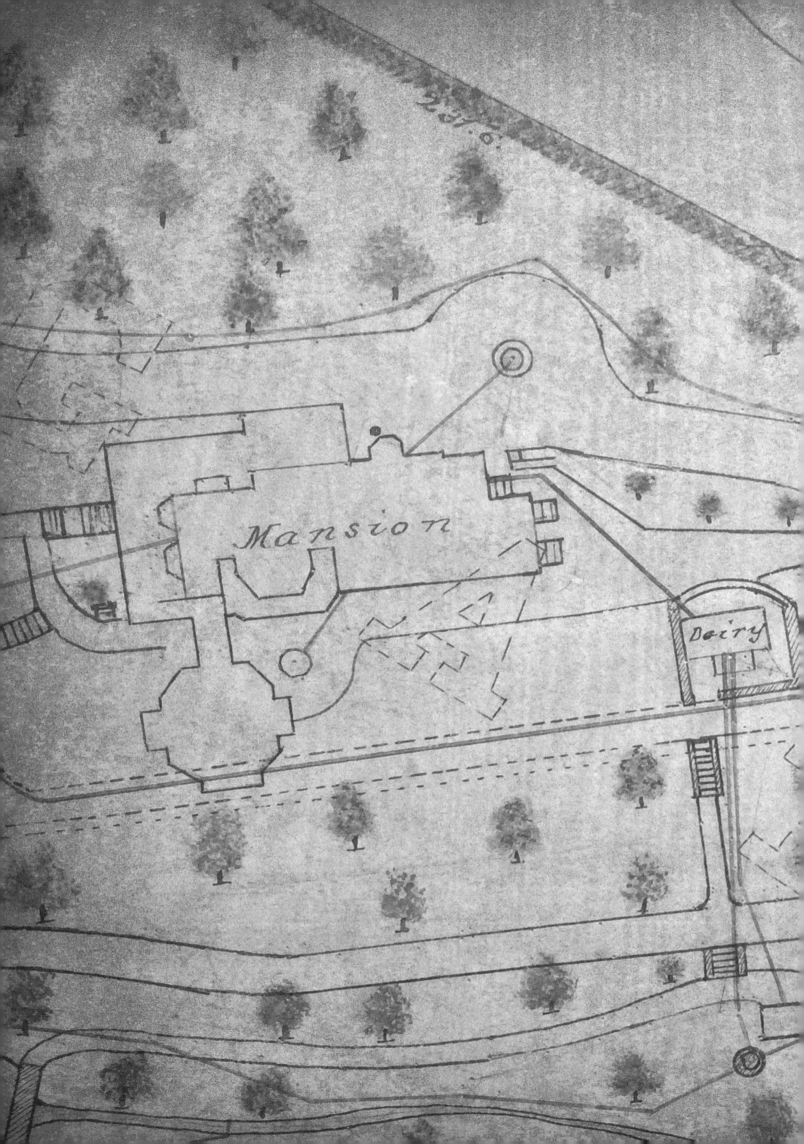

Baltimore's ascent to prominence as one of America's major cities was spawned by its access to the Chesapeake Bay, but more importantly, it was the invention of the railroad that made its success possible. The Baltimore & Ohio Railroad, along with other railroad lines, linked the city with the surrounding rich farmlands, as well as those in the Ohio Valley. It was the railroad that brought the city into an industrial age powered by steam, bringing about the development of textile factories along the Jones Falls valley and iron and machine works in Canton. Baltimore survived

1860-1900:
A Great City Arises

the Civil War unscathed and entered an even greater period of industrial growth. The city expanded into the countryside, absorbing estates and farmland. There, great city mansions were built for the newly wealthy who had created a variety of businesses in the city. Elite neighborhoods surrounding squares like Mount Vernon were created at this time. Factories of brick and iron sprung up all over Baltimore, manufacturing a vast array of products from machine parts to enamelware to ready-to-wear clothing. The architecture of this period, especially for residences, followed the national trends that came and went—Stick style, Shingle style, High Victorian Gothic, and Richardsonian Romanesque. The city understood that with this vast expansion came the need for open space for its citizens to relax and breathe fresh air, and it created a park system anchored by Druid Hill Park. By the end of the nineteenth century, Baltimore was an industrial powerhouse with one newspaper boasting that "It is doubtful if any other large city of the United States shows an equal diversification in its industrial standing."

RUSCOMBE MANSION

In nineteenth-century Baltimore, rich men escaped the heat and humidity of the city by building themselves country estates. They would still have a city residence downtown close to their place of business, but on weekends and for weeks at a time in the summer they would retreat to their mansions. Isaac Tyson Jr. was a Quaker businessman who became the world's largest producer of chromium, a hard, brittle gray metal that is naturally found combined with iron and oxygen in a mineral called chromite. Tyson had found large deposits of the mineral in Baltimore County in 1808 and made a fortune, especially after the original source in Siberia was mined out. After his death in 1861, his sons Jesse and James inherited the business. With all that wealth, they did what rich men of Baltimore did at that time: built country estates for themselves.

Both were located in what was then Baltimore County, and they were next door to each other. Jesse's estate was called Cylburn (extant and now part of the Cylburn Arboretum), which means "cool vale," and James named his mansion Ruscombe, meaning "brown hill." Each built a grand mansion on his land. For his house, James Tyson hired Joseph F. Kemp as the architect. Kemp is best known today for Camden Station, which sits next door to Oriole Park. Using the most popular style of the period, he designed a 20-room Italianate villa with a two-story, 50-foot-square main block topped by a belvedere and surrounded by a balcony. Wide doors opened up onto porches on its south and east sides. Instead of being built in wood frame and clad with stucco that was scored to look like stone, Ruscombe was constructed of native stone.

James raised his family there from 1866 until 1879, until he moved to Vermont, where another company chromite mine was located. In 1887, he sold the mansion and 37 acres to a retired attorney from Chicago, and it remained in his estate until 1948, when it was sold to the Bais Yaakov School for Girls, an Orthodox Jewish school. When a four-alarm fire destroyed the roof and part of the mansion in 1955, the school fought condemnation efforts by the city and rebuilt Ruscombe. When the school moved in 1971, it sold the building to Baltimore City, which leased it to the Waldorf School until 1997.

PROPERTY OVERVIEW

Property Name: Ruscombe Mansion

Address: 4901 Springarden Drive, Baltimore, Maryland 21209

Date Built: 1866

Date Restored: 2009

Architectural Style: Italianate

Original Architect: Joseph Kemp

Original Use: Residence of James Tyson

Current Use: Offices

Developer: Stone Mansion, LLC (Azola Family)

Contractor: Azola & Associates, Inc.

Architect: Azola & Associates, Inc.

Engineers: Carroll Engineering, Inc., Skarda & Associates, Inc.

Awards: Historic Preservation Award—Baltimore Heritage, 2009

Award of Excellence, Historic Renovation—Home Builders Association of Maryland, 2009

Historic Designation: Baltimore City Landmark, National Register of Historic Places

Ruscombe Mansion, circa 1866

"The angry black vulture attacked."

The inspection of the attic was interrupted by a loud, ear-piercing screech. A vulture appeared from the shadows and attacked. The assault was fended off. The reason for the vulture's rage was sitting in the corner of the attic—two newly laid, grapefruit-sized eggs. The Maryland Department of Natural Resources decreed that no construction could begin until the eggs had hatched and the chicks and mother had flown away, so the project was temporarily mothballed. But a year later, after construction started again, the vulture got back into the attic through a window and laid two more eggs. Work was restricted to the exterior and lower floors.

Vacant for ten years, in 2007 the city solicited bids for the mansion's reuse and awarded the project to the Azola company. When the attic was inspected for the first time, it turned out to be the home of a nesting vulture, who was very angry at the intrusion.

Despite missing its original Italianate roof and belvedere, Ruscombe was listed on the National Register of Historic Places. The mansion itself still had all its walls and rooms and original ten-foot hallways intact. The half-round, arched dormers, signature Italianate eave bracketing, fireplaces, and especially the beautiful exterior stone walls were all in place. After 141 years, the interior still conveyed the scale and proportions of a great mansion, making it very adaptable to a conversion to an office building.

Layers of non-original flooring were removed to restore hardwood flooring, casts were made of the existing plaster moldings for replication, and suspended ceilings were torn out to reveal the original plaster ceiling heights. Historic photos of the interior allowed the original grand stair to be re-created. All the interior wood trim was saved and then used as a template for the new trim. The basement, where the servants had toiled, was not a dank, low space. Instead it had a nine-foot ceiling and two rows of arched stone walls, the latter of which supported the floor framing above. The basement was transformed into a handsome office suite with brick floors. Even the vulture's favorite nesting ground in the attic became a pleasant usable space, lit by a set of triple half-round arched windows and round-top dormers.

Before and after servants quarters and kitchen wing

Above: New offices in basement Below: Before and after attic (vulture's lair)

Resident vulture's perch

People like to work in historic buildings because they are one-of-kind workplaces, and Ruscombe, now called the Stone Mansion, leased up quickly. But not everyone liked the new use of Ruscombe Mansion. With the tenants moved in, the mother vulture paid a visit. She broke through the window screen that had served for many years as her entry to her attic nesting place, scaring half-to-death the woman in her workstation right next to it.

The vulture is still seen circling Ruscombe from time to time.

PIMLICO & THE MARYLAND JOCKEY CLUB

Horse racing was once America's passion. On a typical day in the racing season, thousands would attend the races. In Victorian times, it was a social event—ladies and gentlemen would park their carriages in the track's infield and have luncheon, complete with champagne, before watching and wagering on the afternoon racing card. Into the twentieth century, daily attendance at the nation's tracks averaged into the thousands. At the prestigious high-purse trophy races, tens of thousands would fill the stands to cheer their horses on. Standing along the rail and seeing the horses thunder to the finish line was one of the sport's most exciting experiences. A 100-pound jockey trying to control a 1,200-pound horse is still considered one of the most difficult athletic feats in all of sports.

Maryland's rich horse-racing legacy began in 1743 with the founding of the Maryland Jockey Club, America's oldest sporting association. The first recorded race in Annapolis was held in the same year and won by Dungannon, a thoroughbred racehorse imported from England. Racing continued in the state up to the start of the Revolutionary War. In fact, George Washington, an aficionado with a gambling habit, often attended the races. The Maryland Jockey Club continued under a new charter approved by Congress in 1830, but because of the growing economic status of Baltimore City, its operations were shifted there.

Baltimore's most famous racetrack, Pimlico, opened on October 25, 1870, in its present location near Northern Parkway and Park Heights Avenue in Baltimore City. Over 12,000 people attended the opening. It would be America's second oldest racecourse after Saratoga in Upstate New York. The thoroughbred racehorse Preakness won the Dinner Party Stakes, Pimlico's first stakes race held on opening day. In 1873, when Pimlico staged its first race

PROPERTY OVERVIEW

Property Name: Pimlico & the Maryland Jockey Club

Address: 5201 Park Heights Avenue, Baltimore, Maryland 21215

Date Built: 1870

Date Renovated: 1995–2000

Architectural Style: Victorian, Twentieth-Century Modern

Original Architect: John R. Niernsee

Original Use: Thoroughbred Horse Racetrack

Current Use: Thoroughbred Horse Racetrack

Owner: De Francis Family (1984–2002)
De Francis & Magna Entertainment (2002–2007)
Stronach Group (2007–Present)

Engineer: Martin Azola, P.E., 1995–2000

Historic Designation: Contributing Resource—Baltimore City National Heritage Area

American Pharaoh at Pimlico, Triple Crown Winner 2015

for three-year-old horses, they named the race Preakness in honor of its first stakes race winner. The Preakness would become the second jewel in the Triple Crown of thoroughbred horse racing and bring Pimlico international recognition.

Pimlico held one of the most famous match races ever in 1877. Thoroughbred racehorses Parole, Ten Broeck, and Tom Ochiltree ran the race that had been so anticipated. Both houses of Congress were adjourned so members could attend. Parole won by fourth lengths. To this day, a gold bas-relief depiction of the finish of that race greets visitors on the exterior end wall of the Clubhouse.

In 1873, one of Pimlico's most beloved and distinctive edifices was built. Designed by John R. Niernsee, architect of Johns Hopkins Hospital and many other prominent Baltimore buildings, the Victorian-style clubhouse, with its wide veranda and famous weathervane, became the favorite place to watch a race while eating and drinking Pimlico's fine, quality fare (especially the famous chicken salad). Because racing was a social event, people always dressed up for the occasion; woman dressed to the nines in beautiful dresses and hats, and men wore tailored English racing tweeds.

During the racing season, people would travel daily in carriages through Druid Hill Park and up Greenspring Avenue to the track. A rail spur created by the Western Maryland Railroad at its Arlington stop took racing fans directly to the grandstand. Racing in America had its ups and downs, but Pimlico managed to prosper in good times and in bad. A key turning point in American horse racing came with the introduction of the pari-mutuel betting machine, which challenged the traditional shady bookie and his chalkboard at the track. Also of note, Pimlico was the first track to use an electronic starting gate.

Despite all the changes going on in American life, horse racing remained quite popular. The "Sport of Kings" became a passion for the average man and woman, especially because the races were being broadcast on a new invention called the radio. Magically, a fan could be transported thousands of miles away to Santa Anita or Churchill Downs. Many a Baltimore businessman would cut out of work in the afternoon to watch the races at Pimlico. In 1938 Pimlico's most legendary match race took place between Seabiscuit and Triple Crown winner War Admiral. The Biscuit won the 1-3/16 mile race by four lengths, setting a track record. Later, other Maryland tracks, such as Laurel Park and Bowie, opened to meet the demand for the sport.

As the years went by, Pimlico added facilities, including a glass-enclosed grandstand, as well as barns, parking lots, and housing for backstretch workers, all needed for the day-to-day operations of the track. The famous clubhouse was completely restored in 1956 to the delight of fans, who felt it represented a more refined time in Pimlico history than the 1940s industrial-type grandstand that had been there earlier. However, a huge emotional blow to Pimlico fans came in 1966 when the clubhouse—with some of the track's memorabilia—burned down. "All that tradition going up in smoke," said one fan who had witnessed the fire.

A pivotal moment in horse racing came in 1970. Until then, off-track betting (OTB) had been allowed only in Nevada, but the State of New York passed legislation to allow it. Instead of actually going to the track to place a bet and then watch the races, one could place a bet in an off-track betting parlor in their neighborhood and watch the results there. Maryland and other states would adopt this new wagering method as well. OTB greatly increased the betting revenue, but at the same time it took away the need to go to the track. Instead of thousands in attendance cheering the horses on, the huge grandstands were largely empty during the racing season. Except for major racing events like the Preakness, Pimlico and other American tracks came to have a deserted feel. The social event

Above: Original clubhouse Below: Post-fire clubhouse before 1995 renovations began

"Old Hilltop—but there's no hill."

The track was aptly nicknamed "Old Hilltop" because of a small rise in the infield where people liked to watch the races. In the 1930s, when filming horse races became common in the movie newsreels, the "Old Hilltop" rise in the infield was leveled by Alfred Gwynne Vanderbilt II, president of the Maryland Jockey Club and a leader in creating modern America horse racing as a sport, to allow better film coverage of the backstretch.

experience of horse racing was waning. When television began simulcasting races, patrons who did go to the track stayed behind the grandstand to watch races from all over the world on a battery of TVs.

The introduction of the Maryland Lottery, coupled with a prohibition of slot machines at Maryland tracks, dealt racing another one-two punch. Neighboring jurisdictions enhanced purses with their approved slots revenues and, as a result, many local horse operations elected to make the one hour drive out of state for twice the money. The challenge of operating nineteenth-century facilities in an era that saw new state subsidized football and baseball stadiums didn't help. Before long, a number of Maryland breeders, trainers, and staff relocated their operations to adjacent racing states, leaving local tracks hurting. Something had to be done.

Joseph A. De Francis became president of Pimlico and Laurel Race Courses in 1989, following the untimely passing of his father, Frank De Francis, who had assembled common ownership of the Maryland thoroughbred tracks and OTB parlors. Joe's sister, Karin De Francis, joined him as the senior vice president of public relations and marketing. Together they assembled a first-class management team and set off to level the regional playing field regarding purses, slots, and revenues. Upgrading the facilities was an integral part of their agenda.

An aggressive master plan was developed and Marty Azola, who was now a vice president for the Maryland Jockey Club, began renovations in 1995. At Pimlico, the dark hulking industrial buildings were given a thorough cleaning and fresh coats of white paint. Logos were displayed prominently, including the famous "Pimlico—Home of the Preakness," which greets fans as they enter the facility. Hunter-green awnings, bright yellow-and-white buntings, and multiple new egress structures all improved the exterior aesthetics. The huge aluminum-clad, industrial-looking grandstand was clad in a new, insulated stucco covering, giving it a nice, new scale and pleasing color. Barns were upgraded, infield structures were rebuilt, and trackside markers were renewed.

Inside the 250,000-square-foot facilities at both Pimlico and Laurel, almost every area received a facelift. New food courts were built, bars and dining facilities were renovated, and kitchens upgraded. Banners commemorating all the Preakness winners now lined the aisles, TV displays in the simulcast areas were improved, high rollers' rooms were added, bathrooms were remodeled, and overall infrastructure improved. Backstretch facilities, barns, and on-site staff housing were also repaired and rehabbed.

All in all, over $50 million was spent during the 1995–2000 years to make the built environment of the Maryland Jockey Club more attractive to patrons. Despite best efforts, slots were never approved by the Maryland Legislature for location at the tracks. Instead, casinos were authorized in Maryland, and a sizeable share of their slots revenue was set aside for the depleted horse racing purses. As a result of the considerable efforts of the De Francis family, attendance has increased, and many of the breeders, horsemen, and their operations have returned to Maryland. Preakness attendance at Pimlico continues to set records each year, and it is still the largest and richest sporting event in Maryland, by far.

In 2002, Magna Entertainment, headed by Frank Stronach and his daughter, Belinda, purchased controlling interest in the Maryland Jockey Club and completed their acquisition of the De Francis interests in 2007. The Stronach Group owns other premier racing facilities, including Santa Anita Park, Gulf Stream Park, and Golden Gate Fields. They are committed to attracting new fans and building on the colorful 275-year history of the Maryland Jockey Club.

Grandstand receives new exterior covering.

MARYLAND BUILDING

When one speaks of something extremely rare, an exotic plant or animal species comes to mind—rarely does a building. But a piece of architecture can be extraordinary by its very survival. Buildings, especially those built of wood, can easily deteriorate over time. In Baltimore, for instance, none of the original wooden structures from the city's founding in 1729 have survived.

On a hill within the confines of the Maryland Zoo in Druid Hill Park stands an incredible architectural survivor. The little one-story wood-frame building there was originally the Maryland state pavilion, built specifically for the Centennial International Exposition, America's first world's fair, which celebrated the 100-year anniversary of the signing of the Declaration of Independence. The only other pavilion that survives is Ohio's; except for these two, every structure from that fair has vanished. On a 285-acre tract in Fairmount Park in Philadelphia, 10 million visitors toured more than 200 exhibition halls and pavilions spotlighting the country's industrial achievements in commerce, industry, and the arts and sciences. There, Americans first saw Alexander Graham Bell's newly invented telephone, the Remington typewriter, the Corliss Steam Engine, and Heinz ketchup, plus the actual right arm and torch of the Statue of Liberty. The United States was becoming a world industrial power but was still part frontier—Custer's troops had been massacred just a month after the fair opened.

Maryland's pavilion had a tall, central space showcasing her agricultural, fishing, and mining achievements, including oystering in the Chesapeake Bay, and a display of products made in Baltimore. After the Civil War, the city had become a major industrial and manufacturing city.

Like most of the fair buildings, the Maryland Building, designed by George A. Frederick, the same architect who created Baltimore's City Hall, was built in the Stick style. An extremely popular Victorian style that expressed the "stick" skeleton of wood-frame buildings, Stick style placed an emphasis on overstated machine-made porch posts, eave brackets, and exposed trusswork. When the fair was over in November of 1876, all the buildings were dismantled and carted away from Philadelphia, and they essentially disappeared. But, miraculously, Maryland's

Left: Karl Kranz, EVP for Animal Programs and COO at the Maryland Zoo, "Winnie" the penguin, Tony Azola

PROPERTY OVERVIEW

Property Name: Maryland Building at the Maryland Zoo in Baltimore

Original Address: Fairmount Park in Philadelphia—1876 Centennial Exposition

Current Address: Mansion House Drive, Baltimore, Maryland 21217

Date Built: 1876

Date Restored: 2010

Architectural Style: Stick Style

Original Architect: George A. Frederick

Original Use: Represented the State of Maryland at the 1876 Centennial Exposition

Current Use: Maryland Zoo in Baltimore Administrative Offices

Developer: Maryland Zoo in Baltimore, Donald Hutchinson

Design/Builder: Azola & Associates, Inc.

Engineer: Skarda & Associates, Inc.

Consultant: Matthew Mosca—Historic paint finishes

Awards: Preservation Award for Project Excellence—Maryland Historical Trust, 2010

Award of Excellence—Home Builders Association of Maryland, 2010

Historic Designation: Baltimore City Landmark

Maryland Building, circa 1876

pavilion survived and was rebuilt in a new location. In 1886 the 3,584-square-foot cruciform-shaped Maryland Building was reassembled in Druid Hill Park, where the Maryland Zoo had opened in 1876.

Demolition of the building was being considered, but its unique history and the existence of a historic easement prompted a creative restoration plan. In 2008, the building, which was still being used for offices for the zoo, was a forlorn, weather-beaten structure engulfed by vegetation that had greatly accelerated its complete paint failure. But for a 132-year-old building, it had no catastrophic structural rot, no termites, no foundation settlement, and most import-ant, its 12-foot-high doors and double-hung windows were intact. Because there were no gutters, some parts of the building, including the rear porch, which had been exposed to cascading water, had rotted. The Azola company project scope included complete paint removal and repainting, rotten deck replacement, repair of the original tin standing-seam roof, clearing out of all the encroaching vegetation, and replacement of some exterior wood ornamentation, such as the finials and porch balusters.

The repainting was an enormous effort in itself because of the multiple layers of paint on the complex ornamenta-tion and the exterior horizontal beadboard cladding. The condition of the exterior warranted complete paint removal, a messy, hard, painstaking process, and it was decided that an electric heat gun would yield the best results on such a heavy paint buildup. Looking like a heavy-duty hair dryer, the gun blows hot air, causing a paint blister to form. The paint is then scraped off with a putty knife. The process took ten months to complete.

Another important aspect of the repainting was the historic paint analysis of the Maryland Building. When the project began, the entire building had been painted a dull yellow, a completely different color from the original. The architecture of the Stick style in the 1870s typically had polychrome color schemes with as many as six colors used. Matthew J. Mosca, an historic paint finishes consultant, was called in to do a museum-quality paint-finish examination. Collecting 40 samples and using photomicrography—print photos taken through a microscope—132 years' worth of paint layers were uncovered. A reconstruction of the historic finishes was made, revealing the vivid colors originally used. The metal roof, which was originally red, did not have to be replaced, but one odd leak, caused by a bullet lodged in one of the metal panels, was repaired.

Top: South wing before Bottom: South wing after

Before   *After*

Truss repair

Bees Peel Paint.

The paint on the wood exterior of historic buildings deteriorates for a number of reasons—constant exposure to the elements, ultraviolet rays from the sun, high humidity —but rarely because of honey. The Maryland Building was peeling paint in part because of a six-foot-high beehive inside one of its stud walls. The massive amount of honey in it had completely saturated the wood.

Below: Rotten rear deck and railing Far below: After restoration

Carpentry repair on a historic building, especially a Stick-style structure, is a specialized craft, making it difficult to find the necessary skilled workers. But some were found, including five Amish carpenters from Lancaster County, Pennsylvania, who re-created the missing exposed truss over the main entry door. An industrial shaper was even purchased, and six custom knives were made to cut the complicated exterior trim replacement pieces. The rear and front porches were replaced in tongue-and-groove mahogany, an almost indestructible tropical wood.

When the project was finished in 2010, the rare little survivor had been transformed from a peeling, bland-colored shack back into a beautiful, polychrome structure exhibiting the detail and craftsmanship of one of the most original American architectural styles of the Victorian Age.

SOLOMON'S CORNER

One of Baltimore's finest institutions is Johns Hopkins University. Founded in 1876 from a $3.5 million bequest by Baltimore merchant Johns Hopkins, the school revolutionized American college education by using the German university model dedicated to research and graduate training. Prior to its founding, graduate education—getting a Master's or Doctorate degree—didn't exist in the United States. Hopkins became the model of the modern research university, emphasizing the holistic combination of research and studies dedicated to the discovery of knowledge. Future United States president Woodrow Wilson received one of the first PhD degrees (in political science) from Hopkins in 1886.

When people walk through the beautiful Homewood campus, located at Charles and 33rd Streets, they assume that this is the original campus. But Homewood was the university's second campus, the first being located in downtown Baltimore between Howard and Eutaw Streets and Centre and Monument Streets. That location was actually not the one Hopkins had had in mind for his university; he had wanted it on the grounds of his estate, Clifton, in northeast Baltimore. Not a trace of the Howard Street campus survives, but the birthplace of American graduate studies began there. Constructed from 1885 to 1898, the campus was a collection of Romanesque Revival buildings designed mostly by E. F. Baldwin, one of Baltimore's most prolific and important late-nineteenth-century architects.

In the mid-1890s, it was apparent, given the success of the Johns Hopkins University, that they would need a lot more space than was available around Howard and Eutaw Streets. It was in a Mount Vernon mansion at the northeast corner of Calvert and Biddle Streets that one family envisioned, and largely made possible, the new home for Johns Hopkins University.

In 1893 Robert Brent Keyser, an investor in the Baltimore & Ohio Railroad and owner of the Baltimore Copper Smelting & Rolling Company, purchased the marble mansion of Mr. Solomon Corner at 1201 North Calvert Street, which was known as "Solomon's Corner." Built in 1877, this was considered Corner's country house because, at that time, Mount Vernon was mostly rural land. Keyser bought the adjoining house and converted both properties

PROPERTY OVERVIEW

Property Name: Solomon's Corner

Address: 1201 North Calvert Street, Baltimore, Maryland 21202

Date Built: 1877

Date Restored: 2000

Architectural Style: Richardsonian Romanesque

Original Architect: Charles Cassell

Original Use: Residence of Solomon Corner, and then William B. Keyser

Current Use: Offices of Brown Capital Management

Owner: Eddie C. and C. Sylvia Brown Family I, LLC

Design/Builder: Azola & Associates, Inc.

Awards: Preservation Project Award Maryland Historical Trust, 2000

Preservation Project Award—Baltimore Heritage, 2000

Historic Designation: Contributing Resource to the Mt. Vernon Place Historic District, National Register of Historic Places

Exterior marble stone restoration

into a 50-room Richardsonian Romanesque–style mansion. The exterior of 1203 North Calvert was redone to match 1201, with rough-faced marble and two-story swell-front oriel windows topped by intricately detailed wrought-iron railings. The entrance, which was originally on Biddle Street, was shifted to the Calvert Street side. The interior was lavish, with ornamental plasterwork, fireplaces with carved stone surrounds, and wood paneling. The salient feature of the interior was a colossal spiral stair with wrought-iron railings below a domed skylight.

In that impressive interior gathered many of the richest and most influential men of Baltimore, men who would plan the future of Johns Hopkins University. William Keyser, the father of Robert, had joined the first president of Hopkins, Daniel Coit Gilman, on a yachting excursion on the Chesapeake Bay in the fall of 1894. Gilman explained to Keyser that the Howard Street campus was no longer adequate and that new classroom buildings, libraries, and laboratories had to be built. He asked him to lead the effort to find the university a new home. For the next ten years, William Keyser and other prominent Baltimoreans worked to find a parcel of land. The location of the new campus would be in what was then the countryside near his cousin William Wyman's Homewood estate. By the time William Keyser died in 1904, a tract of 180 acres had been assembled. Robert Keyser took over the Homewood

project from his father in 1903, when he was elected president of the university board of trustees, a position he held until 1926. Out of his own pocket, he hired Frederick Law Olmsted to consult on the site planning of the campus. In 1915, Hopkins's new home opened, anchored by what would become the university's most famous building, Gilman Hall. Today Homewood is considered one of the most beautiful college campuses in America.

Shortly after Keyser died in 1927, the mansion was sold and then converted into doctors' offices. It was then sold in 1978, becoming a private residence again. The years hadn't been kind to "Little Hopkins," as it had been nicknamed: its windows were rotted out, the copper oriel window roofs were leaking badly, the electrical system was out of date, and the steam piping had leaked everywhere. In 2000, when the mansion was sold to businessman Eddie C. Brown, the founder of Brown Capital Management, the second oldest African American investment company in America, a complete exterior and interior renovation was undertaken to create a headquarters for the firm. Brown had a special appreciation for historic architecture and wanted the mansion to be preserved as much as possible. Over 24,000 square feet of interior space was restored by the Azola company for modern office use, seven fireplaces were made usable again, the original wood and plasterwork was restored, and all new air-conditioning, electrical, and

The lobby

New stairwell structure

Original elevator machinery, 1911

Spiral marble stair with iron railing

plumbing systems were installed. The original residential elevator Keyser had installed was refurbished to working order. The interior had suffered greatly with the installation of additional plumbing lines for the medical offices, and rooms had been cut up with drywall cubicles and plastic paneling installed over original paneling.

When dealing with the rehab of historic buildings, the phrase "bringing it up to code" always arises, necessitating negotiations with city fire and building officials to make the building safe, while also preserving its important historic features. The great spiral stair remained intact, but to comply with modern fire safety codes, a new mechanical smoke-exhaust system had to be installed, as well as an additional egress stair built where the servants' stair once stood.

Brown Capital Management could have moved its business anywhere for a far lower cost. But a unique commitment was made by Eddie C. Brown and his wife, C. Sylvia, to save the residence and restore it to the days when Robert Keyser used to meet with the rich and influential in his parlor to make Johns Hopkins University the new model of college education in America. Like the Keysers, the Browns became the new generation of philanthropists and benefactors helping Baltimore and its educational institutions—while also preserving the city's architectural heritage in Mount Vernon.

ST. PAUL'S HOUSE

Except for nursing and teaching, there were few job opportunities for literate women in the nineteenth century. Then came a machine invented in 1876 by Christopher Latham Sholes: the typewriter. Prior to that invention, the business world was completely male dominated, down to the position of office boy. But the typewriter eased the entry of women into this formerly masculine world. They eventually became stenographers and typists in businesses of all types because they were reliable and skilled at typing—more so than men. Starting out on a typewriter sometimes led to advancement to low-level managerial positions.

These new "working women" in America's cities were young—eighteen to twenty-four—and single. But they didn't want to live at home anymore and wanted to be on their own. Marriage and children could wait. This attitude transformed the working world. Women had been factory workers, but now they were an essential part of the expanding office bureaucracy that the nation's massive industrial growth required.

But the city was viewed as a dangerous place for a women, full of evil men and liquor. Mothers tried desperately to dissuade their daughters from leaving home. The women would find lodging in the city either living by themselves in a boarding house or in an apartment flat (a new building type of the time) with roommates. The officials at St. Paul's Church, the oldest Episcopal church in Baltimore (1739), had an idea. They needed office space for church administration and meetings, but why not provide rooms on the upper floors for working women? Then they would have a safe, clean place to live. Mothers would sleep soundly knowing their daughters were under the watchful eye of St. Paul's to keep them out of harm's way. So, in 1885, St. Paul's hired architect T. Buckler Ghequiere to design St. Paul's House at 309 Cathedral Street, for exactly that purpose.

The four-story brick building Ghequiere designed was anchored by a tower at its north end with tall, half-round

PROPERTY OVERVIEW

Property Name: St. Paul's House

Address: 309 Cathedral Street, Baltimore, Maryland 21202

Date Built: 1885

Date Restored: 1985

Architectural Style: High Victorian Gothic

Original Architect: T. Buckler Ghequiere

Owner: St. Paul's Episcopal Church, founded in Maryland in 1692

Original Use: Single Women's Housing

Current Use: Offices

Developer: Azola Development Corp.

Contractor: Martin P. Azola & Associates, Inc.

Architect: Lawrence J. Link Jr.

Engineer: Skarda & Associates, Inc.

Awards: Grand Prize—Renaissance '85, National Association of Homebuilders, 1985

Oh, what a mess inside.

arched windows and decorative brick and terra-cotta work, probably influenced by Frank Furness, a great Philadelphia architect practicing at the time. The roof was of slate with dormers, and the transom at the main entry was embellished with a beautiful iron screen. Wide oak-paneled double doors led to the entry foyer. Ghequiere's main stair, which was made of iron, was definitely influenced by Furness, using his signature punched-hole openings in the metal guards of the side railing. The fireplaces throughout the building, which were essential for heat, were also quite ornate. The interior rooms were simply adorned with painted trim and wood floors.

One hundred years later, St. Paul's House had become a wreck. Building code violations were piling up, and repairs were draining church coffers. The city condemned the building as unfit for habitation. Several ideas for saving the building fell through, and there was talk of tearing it down. But one very innovative idea that wouldn't cost the church a penny saved the day. St. Paul's House could be leased to a developer for 30 years who would then do the renovation and in turn, sublease part of the building to the church. The rest of the space would become offices that could be leased out by the developer. Another benefit for the developer was that the project would also be eligible for federal historic tax credits, an additional source of revenue.

The renovation, by the Azola company, took only eight months, transforming the 13,700-square-foot building into

New elevator and lobby

Victorian details abound

a modern office space while retaining most of the historic features, such as the windows and the interior trim. Lawrence J. Link Jr. was the architect who designed the project. Each floor had a kitchen and a bathroom, while the rear porches were glassed in to create extra space. A spiral stair was installed in the tower leading to a space that became a fourth-floor office suite. All new mechanical, electrical, and plumbing systems were installed, as was an elevator. A Federal-style addition, built in 1924, was also rehabbed. About 1,500 square feet of the first floor was for the use of the church, basically at no charge, because the developer's lease paid a bit more than the church's office rent.

When the $500,000 renovation was finished, this Victorian-style building was saved from demolition. No one had ever done such a development partnership with a church in Baltimore.

St. Paul's House is no longer a refuge for single, working women who need looking after; in fact, some of the tenants in the building are women who own their own businesses.

A room of its own.

When T. Buckler Ghequiere designed St. Paul's House in 1885, a new stage in the evolution of domestic design had occurred with the inclusion of a "bathroom." House dwellers were no longer forced to use an outdoor privy but could use a water closet, made possible by adequate water supply piped to individual buildings. Since privacy was a requirement, the device had its own separate room, which was soon joined by another modern convenience: the bathtub. The working women living in St. Paul's House would share a communal bathroom, but the remaining fixture, the sink, would be included much later. Personal washing was done in one's room with a basin and a pitcher of water.

Offices for St. Paul's Episcopal Church

THE FEDERAL PARK

In the early 1730s, French scientist Rene Réaumur was walking through the woods and came upon a wasp's nest. Instead of avoiding it, he took a closer look. The gray shell of the nest was made from wood fibers, he realized. The wasps would chew wood into a pulp and create a paper-like shell. That observation changed the history of the world: a new method of papermaking was discovered. Parchment had been created from animal hides or mostly from pulped rags. Recycling is thought to be a modern concept, but taking rags and recycling them into paper had gone on for centuries. All over the world, ragpickers would drive their horse and wagon through town and city streets, collecting rags. But using rags was expensive, which in turn made paper expensive, which then made books expensive. Working off Réaumur's observation, by the late-nineteenth century, machines were invented to convert pulp wood into paper called newsprint, for a fraction of the cost of rag paper. Books became mass-produced and cheaper, school-children used notebooks instead of chalk and slate, and newspapers could increase their number of pages.

By the 1880s, papermaking was a very profitable business, so George F. Jones built a paper mill in the Federal Hill section of Baltimore, which overlooked the harbor. The name of the neighborhood came from a celebration in 1789 of Maryland's ratification of the new "Federal" constitution. Until the late 1970s, it was a working-class neighborhood, and many residents worked in factories and industries surrounding the nearby harbor or in Federal Hill itself, such as Bethlehem Steel on the east side of the hill. Building a factory in the midst of row houses was a common (and welcome) occurrence. Then, by the 1960s, the industries gradually disappeared, setting Federal Hill on the path to decline. But the introduction of the Baltimore City Dollar Homes program, initiated to rehabilitate row houses in the Otterbein section of the neighborhood, ignited interest in renovating historic buildings, especially among baby boomers who wanted to live in the city. Reinvestment in the neighborhood came quickly, and it became one of the first neighborhoods in Baltimore to be gentrified.

PROPERTY OVERVIEW

Property Name: The Federal Park

Address: 327 Warren Avenue, Baltimore, Maryland 21230

Date Built: 1890

Date Restored: 1988

Architectural Style: Vernacular

Original Architect: Unknown

Original Use: Paper Mill

Current Use: Residential Condominiums

Developer: Azola Development Corp.

Contractor: M. P. Azola & Associates, Inc.

Architect: Burns & Geiger, Richard Burns

Historic Designation: Contributing Resource to the Federal Hill Historic District, National Register of Historic Places

The redevelopment of the Inner Harbor was another key catalyst to Federal Hill's second life. Being listed on the National Register of Historic Places in 1970 and receiving federal historic tax credits spurred the development and helped to fund income-producing renovations, especially on former industrial sites.

In the 1920s the original paper mill building was sold as a warehouse to Shofer's Furniture, a merchant established in Federal Hill in 1914 and that is still there to this day. In 1986 the building was sold to the Azola company, who wished to convert the building into twelve condominiums. With the phenomenal success of Federal Hill's transformation, there was no more vacant land and no more large buildings to recycle. The new project was named the Federal Park. The interior space of the three-story utilitarian building with two-foot-thick brick walls was recycled into two- and three-bedroom units that included the mill's original high ceilings, window openings, and wood flooring. Indoor parking for all occupants was provided on the ground floor. The concept was to retain the building's industrial character while also providing high-end amenities like luxurious bathrooms and kitchens, fireplaces, marble foyers, and private decks or balconies. Even the common areas such as the hallways, elevator, and lobby were done with a high level of elegance. The condominiums were designed by architect Richard Burns.

Because of the building's location on Warren Avenue, which is directly across from Federal Hill Park, a fourth story was added for penthouse residences. The design of the addition was in keeping with the character of the building. Looking out from the addition, residents are awed by the sweeping panorama of the city skyline and the Inner Harbor. The view had completely changed from Federal Hill's days as a working-class enclave. Those former residents looked out onto factories, shipping terminals, and warehouses, now all gone except for the Domino Sugar factory building. Today the once bustling, working Inner Harbor is essentially a tourist attraction, but the residents of the Federal Park can live above all that and enjoy the most spectacular view in Baltimore.

Baltimore skyline vista

"My God, what an incredible view."

During the hugely successful development of Baltimore's Inner Harbor, most people rushed to buy residences downtown with a view looking over the waters of the harbor. The bustling port and industrial buildings provided the always active background. However, the best vista was actually the opposite. Looking back across the harbor at the mass of downtown structures from high atop Federal Hill was far more spectacular. Only a handful of buildings bordering the park provided this enjoyable view. And until the recent proliferation of high-rise buildings in the Harbor East neighborhood, the Federal Park project boasted the undisputed best views in town. Many say it still does.

DEVON HILL

The Shingle style was the apogee of America's architectural creativity. For a brief period from the 1870s to the mid-1890s, there was a truly American style that was inspired by the nation's seventeenth-century Colonial houses. Typically used on large, rambling houses, naturally weathering wood shingle cladding would appear to flow across surfaces, wrapping bay windows and columns and covering steep roofs and wide dormers. The style came after the Queen Anne style but was more horizontal, with almost no ornamentation. Its impact came from powerful massing and uniform color of the shingles set atop a stone foundation. Because it was used frequently for buildings in resorts and for country houses, it was called the "architecture of the American summer."

That's exactly why the O'Connor family built Idlemont in the 1880s. Wealthy families escaped Baltimore City's hot and humid summers by transplanting themselves and their servants into the countryside of Baltimore County. The O'Connor family constructed their summer house on the crest of a hill so that Idlemont's many tall windows and verandas would capture a constant cool breeze. The architect, who is unknown, included a huge double-deck veranda overlooking a gently sloping hill that had woods and a pond, as well as gardens designed by Frederick Law Olmsted. It provided a magnificent view of the Jones Falls valley to the north.

Though most homes were over 10,000 square feet in size, Baltimore families always referred to them as "cottages." The unusual feature of Idlemont was that instead of being just a summer residence, it actually was the center of a 94-acre self-sufficient farm. A barn for a dairy, the tenant farmer's house, stables, a smokehouse, and root cellar were also built.

The interior layout of a Shingle-style house was groundbreaking as well. American houses had always been a series of rooms closed off by doors. Now the interior space was opened up, flowing together through wide openings between rooms all radiating from a central living hall that had a big fireplace and monumental stair. The flow of continuous space one sees in today's houses originated in the Shingle style. Idlemont had interior spaces sweeping

PROPERTY OVERVIEW

Property Name: Devon Hill

Address: Devon Hill Road, Baltimore, Maryland 21210

Date Built: 1885

Date Restored: 1983

Architectural Style: Shingle Style

Original Architect: Unknown (1905 expansion by Henry Bacon)

Landscape Architect: Frederick Law Olmsted

Original Use: Summer Home

Current Use: Multifamily Residences

Developer: Devon Hill LP (Azola Family)

Contractor: Martin P. Azola, Inc.

Architect: Peterson & Brickbauer

Engineer: Lyon Associates, Inc.

Awards: Grand Prize—Renaissance '84, National Remodeler's Council, 1984

A parlor in the mansion, circa 1890

Original staircase and entry foyer restored

from room to room. The level of intricately carved wood detailing on the interior of "the cottage" stood in contrast to the plain, unadorned exterior of the house. Rooms had floor-to-ceiling paneling, paneled wainscoting, dropped-beam ceilings, and ornate fireplaces.

Idlemont was later sold to Joseph Jenkins, who expanded the original house, including an addition in 1905 designed by Henry Bacon, best known for the Lincoln Memorial in Washington, DC. Five generations of the Jenkins family lived at the newly renamed Windy Gates until it became economically unfeasible to maintain such a large estate. In the early 1980s, the decision was made to sell the property, including the main house. But the Jenkins family didn't want to sell to developers who would raze the house and the rest of the farm structures to subdivide the land for typical suburban houses. They wanted a developer who would preserve as much of the property as possible, so instead of taking the highest bid

for the estate, they organized the sale as a design competition that emphasized historic preservation. The property would be sold to the winner.

Estates in the United States that could not be sustained by families any longer experienced different fates. Some, like the Great Gatsby–type mansions on the North Shore of Long Island, were donated to private schools and colleges and survived fairly intact. But the majority became white elephants that sat vacant, were vandalized, or were torn down. With the growing historic preservation movement in the 1980s came the idea of converting the main houses into condominiums. By sensitively subdividing a mansion, a new residential use could be found for them that still preserved their historic integrity. The winner of the design competition, the Azola company, had such a plan, which included a condominium conversion into five units as well as converting the carriage house and stables into housing. The house was so huge

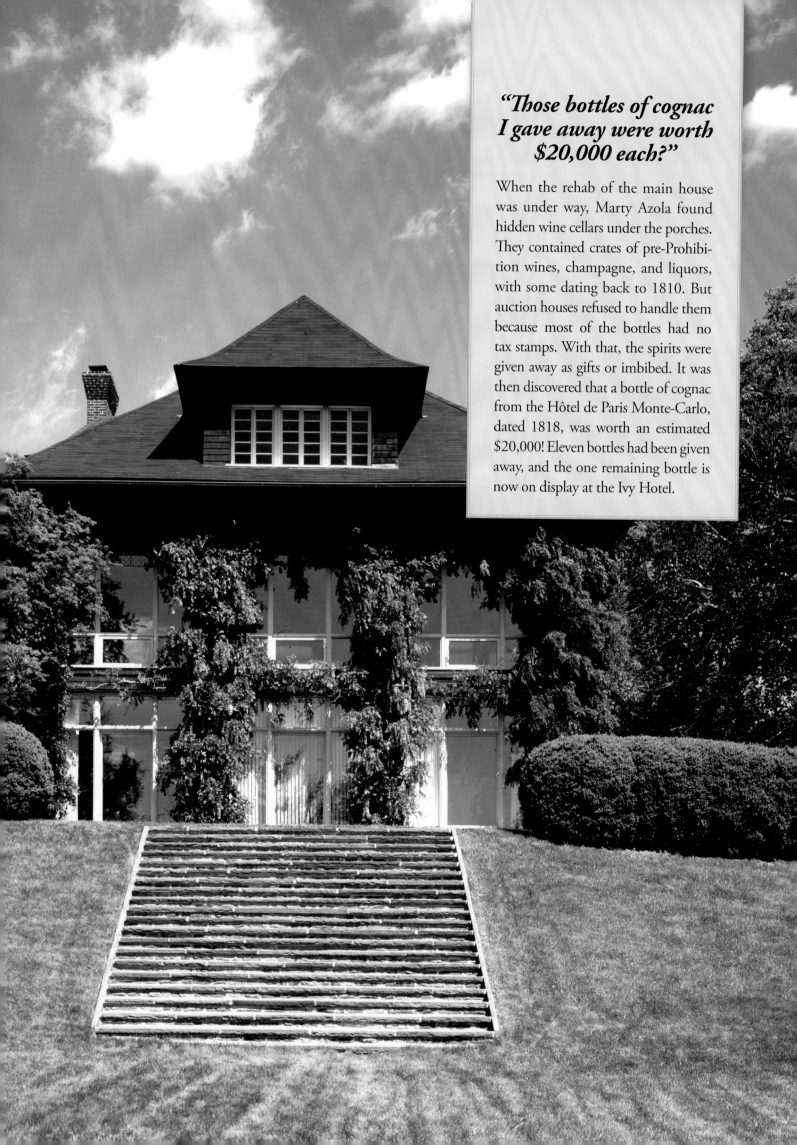

"Those bottles of cognac I gave away were worth $20,000 each?"

When the rehab of the main house was under way, Marty Azola found hidden wine cellars under the porches. They contained crates of pre-Prohibition wines, champagne, and liquors, with some dating back to 1810. But auction houses refused to handle them because most of the bottles had no tax stamps. With that, the spirits were given away as gifts or imbibed. It was then discovered that a bottle of cognac from the Hôtel de Paris Monte-Carlo, dated 1818, was worth an estimated $20,000! Eleven bottles had been given away, and the one remaining bottle is now on display at the Ivy Hotel.

Olmsted gardens overlook the Jones Falls valley.

that the subdivision produced five condominium units of almost 2,000 square feet, the average size of a detached house. Three new houses that were historically compatible with the Shingle-style main house were constructed on the property, providing another 27 units. The architect, Peterson & Brickbauer, preserved the intricate interior detailing, including the house's main staircase. They assigned new functions to rooms: dining rooms became living rooms; bedrooms were converted into kitchens. New mechanical, plumbing, and electrical systems that would not disturb the interior historic fabric had to be installed in each unit. Because the house and the grounds of an estate are a historic ensemble, the development plan preserved both. Olmsted's garden, the woods, and the pond were successfully integrated into the site plan. The porches, which overlooked the garden, were enclosed with glass to add more space to the condominium units.

The genius of the Devon Hill (as it was renamed) design was the siting of the buildings to overlook not only the Olmsted gardens, but the Jones Falls valley into Mount Washington, several miles away. Even the ground-level units had unobstructed views. Prior to construction, the first buyer asked what the view would be like from her balcony. The developer invited her to lunch the following day atop a three-story scaffolding placed directly on the spot of her proposed balcony. On that warm, sunny day, they climbed the scaffold, had lunch on the top deck, and marveled at the views. The deal was signed right then and there.

When Devon Hill was completed in 1984, the units sold quickly. Living on top of a hill made the owners feel as if they were isolated in the middle of the countryside, even though Devon Hill was only seven miles from the Inner Harbor of Baltimore.

THE BARN AT WINDY GATES

On summer days, the owners of Idlemont would sit in the shade of their veranda and look down the sweeping hill at their great estate and dairy building. They probably would have never imagined where the cows were being milked would one day become a beautiful home.

Since the estate that became the Devon Hill development was a working farm, there were ancillary buildings around the main house. The sprawling dairy barn, with caretaker's quarters in the oldest separate wing, was one of the largest in Baltimore County. Vacant since 1940, the buildings had basically fallen into ruin. Mice, snakes, and vegetation had overrun the place. But with patience, a limited budget, and some imagination, the U-shaped 8,000-square-foot buildings were transformed into a real home by the Azola company.

Five 40-yard dumpsters of just trash were removed before even beginning the renovation. Although it did have a septic system and drinking-water connection, the electrical wiring was substandard, unsafe, and served by a tiny outdated panel. The plumbing consisted mainly of the watering trough for the animals, terra-cotta pipe storm drainage, an artesian well, and a few hose bibbs. But the quality of workmanship in the construction of the dairy, just a utilitarian farm building, was extraordinary, the work of a real craftsman in the 1880s.

The south wing of the barn became the starting point for the initial renovation into a kitchen, living room, and bedrooms. The major design feature was the glassing in of the covered breezeway between the two buildings to create an entry foyer and a kitchen with a sunny breakfast room that would overlook a stone patio at the rear. Adjacent to the new foyer was the cow-washing stall and the bull's stall, which were converted into a temporary master bedroom and a study. The attic area, which originally served as hay- and feed-lofts and was accessed by doors in the gable ends, became a playroom for children that was accessed from the interior of the house by a ladder to a trapdoor. Later on, the attic roof was bumped up using a square Victorian dormer to create a real master bedroom suite, with a stair

PROPERTY OVERVIEW

Property Name: The Barn at Windy Gates

Address: W. Lake Avenue,
　　Baltimore, Maryland 21210

Date Built: 1885

Date Restored: 1989–2003

Architectural Style: Vernacular

Original Architect: Unknown

Original Use: Dairy Barn

Current Use: Private Residence

Developer: Devon Hill LP (Azola Family)

Contractor: The Azola Family

Architect: Warren Peterson

Interior Design: Tayne and Ronnie Renmark,
　　Richmond, VA

Awards: 1997 Grand Award—Renaissance '97,
　　Remodeling Magazine, 1997

The vacant barn, 1988

Above: Former wash stall turned bedroom   Below: The bull's stall, now den

replacing the ladder. The original feed bins are still in the attic.

The remaining garage and the long section with the milking stalls became a workshop, a one-car garage, and storage space. The architect for the project was Warren Peterson. More recently, the milking stalls in the north wing were converted into a separate loft apartment for guests. The interior plaster there contains Portland cement, used to withstand animal kicking and water from washing. It's so hard that even to hang a picture requires the use of a hammer drill with a carbide masonry bit to make nail holes.

It was important to incorporate some historic features of the dairy, such as keeping the corrugated tin ceiling and the lights from the cow-washing stall. The three-inch-thick heart-pine sheathing in the bull's stall became wainscoting in the study. The board-and-batten exterior was repaired and repainted, and a new shed roof supported by simple square columns was built to shelter the entryway. Some of the original casement wood windows were restored and reglazed with insulating glass. Original stall Dutch doors were rebuilt. Some historic elements in the renovation, like a sliding barn door, were taken from other old barns. The floors were finished with oak plank hardwood. New construction details, like triangular-top doors, kept the ambiance of the dairy. At the end of the living room, a new Rumford fireplace was built with stone salvaged from a historic home in western Maryland that had burned down. One hundred tons of foundation stone from the ruins of a burned barn were also used in the renovation.

Such an extensive renovation wasn't done in a day; it actually took many painstaking years while living in the building the whole time the renovation was going on. But when the project won *Remodeling* magazine's grand prize for adaptive reuse in 1997, a judge exclaimed, "What a nice place to come home to."

Above: Bedroom in the attic Below: Modest addition

Rat-proofing can save energy.

Wherever there's feed and grain stored to feed livestock, there are always going to be rats looking for a snack. The exterior of the dairy barn is clad with heavy one-inch-thick board-and-batten planks, but the eight-inch space between the siding and the interior plaster is filled with two wythes of brick for rat-proofing because rats can't chew through brick. The heavy brick provided a high thermal mass that was excellent for conserving energy. Thermal mass is important to passive solar heating and for absorbing and retaining heat.

THE IVY HOTEL

In the late-nineteenth century, when a wealthy, successful, Baltimore businessman wanted a new home in the city, there was only one place to build it—Mount Vernon. John Gilman, a banker and industrialist, chose to build his city mansion on the southeast corner of Biddle and North Calvert Streets. There, his Gilded Age neighbors in their freestanding mansions and elegantly appointed high-style row houses were among some of the richest people in the nation, let alone Baltimore.

In 1889, Gilman hired one of the premier architects in Baltimore, Charles L. Carson, to design his house. Carson was one of the finest designers in America. He employed Romanesque Revival in his designs, a style characterized by bold arches, deep red brick, and brown sandstone. In *Architectural Record*'s second issue, which came out in 1891, an article entitled "The Romanesque Revival in America" featured many of Carson's buildings. His most acclaimed buildings in the city were the Central Savings Bank, the Equitable Building, and the Mount Vernon Place United Methodist Church. He was quite in demand for Mount Vernon houses; in fact, Carson also designed the mansion directly across from Gilman's.

For Gilman's new home, the architect anchored the building on its corner site with a three-story tower and a slate-covered turret roof (that was nicknamed a "witch's hat"). Streets in Mount Vernon had a hierarchy, so the main entry—a set of stone steps leading to a wide, handsome wood door—was placed on Calvert Street. Throughout this exclusive neighborhood in the late-nineteenth century, a coachman would pull his livery of horses in front of this fine entry to let the owner and his family off. On the less prominent Biddle Street side, Carson used a two-story bay to give prominence to the north facade. In this period, because gas lighting only gave off dim illumination, it was important to have tall, wide windows that would flood the interior with daylight. Servants would close the interior shutters at night and when the owners were traveling or staying in their summer residences to escape the heat and humidity of the city. An unusual feature on the Calvert Street side was a shallow portico framed by short columns on the third floor.

Brick and brownstone restoration

Above: Original stairwell Below: Stairwell and stained glass restored

Like a painter with his palette of colors, an architect has a palette of materials that give color and texture to the interior and exterior of a design. Carson chose a rich, sanded Baltimore red brick for the body of the Gilman Mansion and Seneca stone for the trim and base. Quarried along the Potomac River upstream from Washington, DC, Seneca stone is a red sandstone that is gray in color when cut but turns red when rain moistens its iron-oxide content. The stone, which was used for the Smithsonian Institution's "Castle" on the Mall in Washington, DC, is remarkable in its durability and unique color. But the quarry ceased production in 1901.

The interior of the Gilman Mansion is laid out like a typical city house of the period, with an arcaded inner vestibule leading to a stair hall that connects the reception room, the parlor, and the dining room. A grand staircase with a beautifully carved railing is at the end of the hall, lit by windows made of what they called "cathedral glass." Every business magnate needed his private study from which to retreat from the world, and Carson designed a magnificent one at the end of the first-floor hall for Gilman with parquet flooring, a fine Vermont Verde stone fireplace, and a bow window lined with leaded glass and built-in seating. The interior finishes were expensive hardwoods like quartered oak for the wainscoting in the parlor and mahogany in the study and for the staircase. Bedrooms were on the second and third floors, with servants sleeping in the attic.

The Gilman Mansion is an example of the curious path of ownership by Gilded Age millionaires in Baltimore, and America at large. Often, by the time the expensive, extravagant house was finished, the owner had died or was only able to live in the new house for a few years before his death. Such was the case for John Gilman, who died in 1889, never actually having lived in his house. His widow, Eliza; his widowed daughter, Charlotte Gilman Paul; and Charlotte's son, Gilman D'Arcy Paul, lived in the house until 1896, when they sold it to another wealthy man.

The next owner, William Painter, became very rich from a simple but revolutionary invention that is still used today—the crown bottle cap. Soft drinks like Coca-Cola and Dr Pepper became very popular in the 1880s, but they were only dispensed in drugstores. Beer always came from a tap in a tavern. Carbonated beverages were difficult to bring home because the primitive stoppers used in bottles did not provide a sufficient seal to keep in the carbon dioxide that made them bubbly. Painter, a Quaker born in Montgomery County, Maryland, devised a brilliantly simple design: a metal lid lined with a thin cork disk that was inexpensive

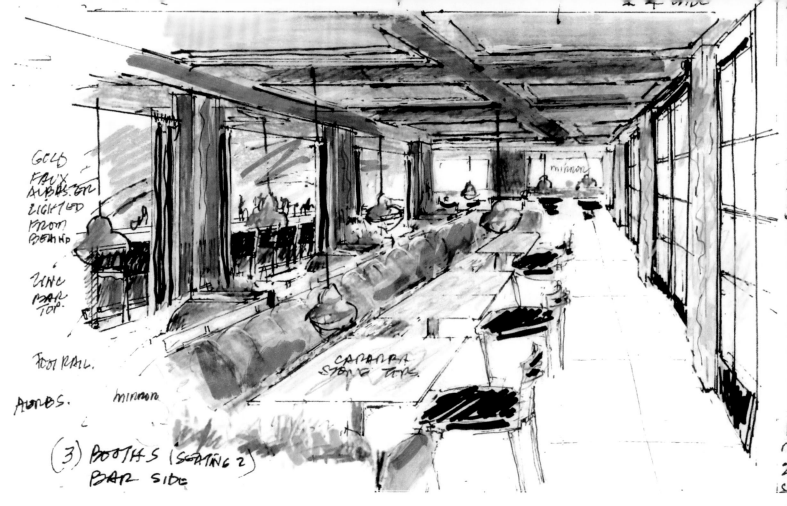

GOLD
FAUX
ALABASTER
LIGHTED
FROM
BEHIND

ZINC
BAR
TOP.

FOOT RAIL.

AURES.   mirrors

(3) BOOTHS (SEATING 2)
BAR SIDE

CABANRA
STONE TOPS.

Above: Design concept for restaurant Magdalena (Joszi Meskan); below: Magdalena open for business, June 2015

and, most important, leak-proof. The caps had a corrugated edge that looked like a crown. Painter, who had invented other ingenious devices like a paper-folding machine and a safety-ejection seat for passenger trains, filed for the patent in 1892 and in 1894 received U.S. Patent No. 468,258 for the bottle cap. That same year he received his patent, he invented the bottle-cap opener.

Painter founded the Crown Cork & Seal Company (now the world's largest bottle-capping company) in Baltimore. But he had to convince bottle makers to make a special neck tip design for the cap to grip when it was pressed onto the bottle. He also had to invent a foot-powered capping device in 1898 that bottlers could use to seal bottles quickly without breaking them. Once the cap was universally accepted, Painter began to make his fortune, and he wanted a city mansion for himself. But instead of building one, Painter bought the Calvert Street house from the Gilman family and lived there until he died in 1906.

The Painters already had a town house less than three blocks away, at 1202 North Charles, but the very much more elegant house at 1129 North Calvert may have been purchased to facilitate the Baltimore debut of their youngest child, Ethel Gilpin Painter. As a debutante, Ethel was introduced to Baltimore society at a luncheon held at the mansion on November 9, 1899, and her "coming out" portrait now hangs in the Hotel Ivy's upstairs dining room.

Above: Tea room looking into the library Below: The new conservatory

Interior designer Joszi Meskan consults with artist Kim Parr.

Mrs. Painter and her oldest child lived primarily in their house in Roland Park after William's death, but when Mrs. Painter's estate was settled after 1918, the mansion was sold to a Johns Hopkins Medical School professor, Dr. Thomas B. Futcher, who lived in, and conducted his practice in, the house from 1920 to 1929.

During the Great Depression, many opulent mansions and row houses where the wealthy once resided were cut up into apartments, or in the case of 1129 North Calvert, converted to medical offices. In 1938, the mansion was purchased by the 1896 Olympic athlete Robert Garrett, of the B&O Railway family, and deeded to the Baltimore City Department of Recreation and Parks, of which Garrett was the longtime chairman of the board. The 1938 sale proved quite fortunate for the fate of the house. The conversion of mansions to apartments often destroyed one-of-a-kind historic features, and many buildings were simply left to decay until deemed unfit for habitation. But the Gilman Mansion escaped that destiny because Baltimore City recognized its architectural significance and left the house basically intact as an un-subdivided office space.

In the 1980s, Baltimore City was under the leadership of Mayor William Donald Schaefer, who spearheaded the Inner Harbor project and many other urban improvements. By 1985, Recreation and Parks had outgrown their space in the mansion, and relocated. Mayor Schaefer envisioned a guest house for dignitaries visiting the city, and to that end two marble-and-brick-faced row houses at 1125 and 1127 North Calvert Street (immediately to the south of the mansion) were purchased. All three buildings were combined to create Government House, which was managed by a private hospitality company. By the early 2000s, the venture was abandoned, and the city put the building up for sale.

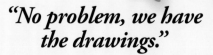

"No problem, we have the drawings."

Sometimes you have luck in a historic rehab when reproducing a building feature. The mansion needed new outside metal grilles that had to match the original ones. The development team contacted the Baltimore iron working firm G. Krug & Son, who had been in business since 1810. Krug said they had done the metal grilles for the original building from 1889 for Charles Carson and still had the shop drawings in their records.

The Ivy before restoration

Suite 7 awaits.

A neighbor directly across Biddle Street, entrepreneur and philanthropist Eddie C. Brown, had his eyes on the mansion. Brown was the founder of Brown Capital Management (BCM) and was well-known to America as a regular panelist for many years on PBS's financial show, *Wall $treet Week with Louis Rukeyser.* The close proximity of Government House to BCM suggested several adaptive reuse scenarios, and the Azola company became involved to help decide the best use for the building in a way that would invest in, and support, the city of Baltimore.

The handmade French Molteni stove

Garrett Hotel Consultants of Charlotte, Vermont, were brought in to determine the feasibility of converting the mansion and adjoining row houses into a very high-end luxury boutique hotel, a hospitality product that Baltimore did not yet have. A world-class hotel was envisioned that would make its guests feel as though the mansion was a private home, and would offer guests a level of service harking back to the Gilded Age, when a mansion had a staff to see to every need of a family and its visitors.

But there was an immense amount of renovation required before that could happen. The mansion itself looked worn-out, with peeling paint on its windows and pollutant soiling on the Seneca stone. The 1985 renovated interior was also dated, but all in all it was still in good condition. When the city did the renovation, the many fireplaces, original wood and mosaic tile flooring, historic doorways, and most of the original architectural detailing were kept. Roof deterioration is often the biggest cause of decay in a historic building, and in this case, the mansion's slate roof had leaked in several places, leading to plaster damage in the rooms below. A very distinctive feature was in the rear, where English ivy completely covered the three-story bay windows like a wall of green. In some places, it was so thick, one could not see through the windows. The wild and rampant ivy gave the building a romantic-ruin air, and the hotel its name.

At first the plan was to work with the existing three buildings to create the new hotel, but once the design team had been assembled, new ideas and directions were considered. The noted Baltimore firm of Ziger/Snead was contracted to design both the renovated original space and an addition in the rear parking lot that would be historically compatible with the mansion in form and materials. The addition would replace a plain, flat-roofed brick addition that had been built along Biddle Street to house a commercial-grade kitchen constructed in the Government House era. And the new walls would enclose an interior garden of lush green space to give guests and diners a respite from the city noise and bustle.

The renovation of a historic building offers a very different set of challenges compared to constructing a building from scratch. One has to work with existing conditions and make the new design work within the confines of many restrictions protecting historic features. Finding the right craftsmen to do high-quality work is another enormous challenge. More than 60 local artisans and specialists were brought in to salvage floors and do restoration work. They replastered walls, repaired the slate roofing, and restored the many doors. Walter Raines spent almost two years meticulously bringing the tired and depleted original oak woodwork on the mansion's first floor back to life. Experts in leaded glass were called in. Of the 140 balusters in the three-story main staircase, 104 needed to be replaced. Mark Supik drew on his expertise in crafting beer tap handles to replicate the original tap handles exactly. Jim Brewster used gold leaf to paint the artful guest room numbers on the door transoms, and hundreds of tiny gold ivy leaves were embossed on the library's leather walls.

In addition, completely new heating, cooling, electrical, and plumbing systems had to be installed without causing any adverse effects on the historic elements. A guest room had to be cooled and heated in an unobtrusive fashion, so no ductwork could be seen. Another aspect of historic renovation is that if you cannot salvage a historic item, you must replace it in kind, meaning that you need to replicate it exactly as it was. Many old fragments had to be measured so that they could be reproduced.

Being a federal historic tax credit project, the design had to be compatible in scale, massing, and material. The connection to the original mansion was crucial. The architect used a flat-roofed connector to join the mansion to a steeply roofed structure that overlooked the garden to the south. They picked up on details from the mansion, including an oculus window, copper gutters and downspouts, a slate-covered shed dormer, and slit windows in the gables. It is a distinctly modern building that harmonizes with the mansion, especially in color and texture, with its real brownstone facing that was quarried in England.

The dining room set up for a business meeting

Interior designer Joszi Meskan of San Francisco was involved with the project from its beginning. Rather than replicating the heavily Victorian-style design of the 1985 renovation, she utilized furnishings, fabrics, art, and accessories, both antique and contemporary, to create public and guest rooms of great verve and elegance in the style of the Aesthetic Movement, appropriate to the building's period. The sourcing for the interiors was jump-started by acquiring the beautiful contents from the 15 rooms of the Inn at National Hall, soon to be converted to offices, in Westport, Connecticut, that Meskan had designed in 1990. "This is not going to be Grandma's house," she had said with conviction. Unless Grandma had been an adventurous and unconventional world traveler with a taste for the exotic and eccentric.

Each of the 18 suites and rooms are individually decorated, and feel like those in a private home. Once cluttered with castaway furniture and other bric-a-brac, they are now havens of light, comfort, and whimsy. As in the renovation of the building itself, local artists and artisans added immensely to the distinctive surroundings. A team of students from Maryland Institute College of Art (MICA) contributed their skills and creativity, hand painting the exteriors of the outdated TV cabinets to create quirky, yet practical, sculptural features; the cabinets now house each guest room's complimentary minibar, and have been christened "barmoires."

As a result of the development team's efforts, the internationally renowned hotel association Relais & Châteaux deemed that both the building and the hotel's operating style qualified it for acceptance into arguably the most exclusive collection of hotels throughout Europe, Asia, and the Americas.

The Ivy Hotel is home to Magdalena—a fine-dining bistro, both informal and thrilling, that is a culinary jewel in Baltimore. The cross-cultural menu is built upon the finest local ingredients and changes with the seasons and the inspiration of the chef. There are five distinctive dining areas at Magdalena: the Garden Room, which looks out onto the Ivy's breathtaking courtyard; the courtyard itself, where you feel like you are dining within a secret garden with its cozy, ivy-covered walls, topiary plants, and fountain; the intimate, romantic Treasury—where sterling and crystal were once kept under lock and key and where welcoming tables now stand under pools of lamplight; the handsome, convivial bar, where diners are welcome to enjoy drinks before moving to their table; and the sumptuous Robert M. Parker, Jr. Wine Cellar, named in honor of the world's foremost wine authority, a native Baltimorean, and a frequent guest at the restaurant. The Ivy is very proud to be the only wine cellar in the world to be permitted to use Mr. Parker's name. The focus of the cellar is superb, small-production American wines, although the Ivy also has a broad selection of unique wines from around the world, as well as dozens of 100-point wines.

The hotel has been a great success. *Travel + Leisure* recognized the Ivy as one of "The Best Hotels on the Planet." *Conde Nast Traveler* included the hotel on their Gold List 2017 and 2018, and *TripAdvisor* consistently rates the Ivy as number 1 of 66 hotels in Baltimore. As one of their guests reflected, "The Ivy felt like the intimately and luxuriously appointed mansion of a friend you wished you had…."

Morning sun floods the dining room at breakfast.

Eddie C. Brown and C. Sylvia Brown

Above: Original unused attic space Below: Suite 17 hideaway

ODD FELLOWS HALL

Networking is thought of as a computer-age concept, but it has been going on in America since the founding of the republic. For centuries, men have joined the Freemasons, the Rotary, or dozens of other fraternal organizations to engage in civic and charitable work—and also to make business contacts. They would be each other's "frater," the Latin word for brother. One of the oldest of these American organizations is the Independent Order of Odd Fellows (IOOF), founded in Baltimore in 1819. The IOOF added "soror," Latin for sister, when they became the first fraternity in America to allow female members in 1851. The Baltimore Grand Lodge built their first Odd Fellows Hall at Gay Street near Fayette in 1831. The Civil War hurt membership nationally, but the Baltimore Lodge held together and eventually outgrew their first home. In 1889 they acquired a parcel on the corner of Saratoga and Cathedral Streets for $42,300 in order to build a new lodge. Designed by the highly regarded Baltimore architect Frank E. Davis, the four-story building, which opened in 1891, is a brick-and-brownstone Romanesque Revival design that incorporates the style's signature feature: huge round arches at the entries. The order eschewed the usual ornate decoration that went with the style "because this was in accordance with the simple character of the order's founder," Thomas Wildey, who was "plain as a pipe stem with a heart as large and sympathetic as the principles of the order."

The interior consisted of large rooms for meetings of neighborhood lodges around Baltimore. Other rooms were used for lodge rituals and for storing their large supplies of ceremonial regalia. The Highcliffe Grand Ballroom was the main interior feature, where big social functions were held. In 1931 the building was altered, the interior done in the Art Deco style. In 1943, during World War II, the building was shared with the USO, becoming the second largest club in the city, with 39,000 servicemen attending each month.

When IOOF moved out of the building in 1976, they literally sold the place lock, stock, and barrel. The building

PROPERTY OVERVIEW

Property Name: Odd Fellows Hall

Address: 300 Cathedral Street, Baltimore, Maryland 21202

Date Built: 1891

Date Restored: 1976

Architectural Style: Romanesque Revival

Original Architect: Frank Davis

Original Use: Grand Lodge of Maryland, Independent Order of Odd Fellows

Adaptive Reuse: Offices

Developer: Investment Properties Company, LP

Contractor: J. R. Azola & Associates, Inc.

Architect: Peterson & Brickbauer

Awards: Restoration Award—Baltimore Heritage, 1978 Building Owners and Managers Association Restoration Award, 1980

Historic Designation: Individually listed on the National Register of Historic Places

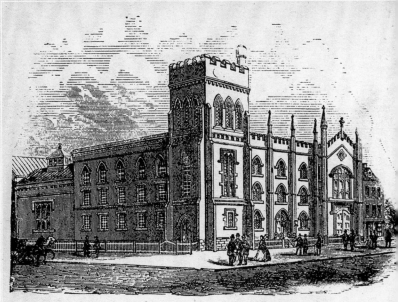

First Odd Fellows Hall in America, Gay Street, 1831.

The second she opened the trunk and saw the skeleton, the lights went out and she screamed in alarm!

The 60,000-square-foot building came with all of the order's furnishings, memorabilia, and kitchen equipment. Over 2,500 pieces of antique furniture had to be inventoried. When Lone Azola began the task, she opened a trunk and found a skeleton at the exact moment the electricity went out, plunging her into total darkness. She was understandably shaken. By the time the inventory was completed, she had discovered 14 skeletons in total. Purchased from the University of Maryland School of Medicine, they were the bones of unidentified Civil War soldiers and may have been used as part of the order's ceremonial rituals.

Massive masonry entrance

had to be cleaned out before the Azola rehab could begin. It was full of thousands of pieces of antique furniture, including pearl-inlaid Brunswick pool tables, player pianos, oak captain's chairs, maple Windsor chairs, roll-top desks, and more. Lodge regalia, robes, hats, and costumes jammed the built-in lockers. Kitchen implements, massive iron and butcher-block tables, Depression glass, and day-to-day tableware were abandoned. The attic was strewn with ancient letters circa 1850, regalia catalogs, and early stamped postcards. All the contents were auctioned for $17,000, which seemed acceptable then.

The building was returned to its 1891 form and converted into an office complex called Cathedral Place. The shell, the windows, and slate roof of the IOOF Hall were restored. New entrance storefronts and public area finishes were created. Interior work included new finishes, and mechanical, plumbing, and electrical systems. The water-source heat-pump system installed for heating and air conditioning was state-of-the-art at the time. Energy from one space could be recaptured in the constantly circulating water loop and used in other spaces without purchasing "new energy." Hiding the truck-sized, heat-rejecting condenser in the basement took some careful engineering and execution. The large original spaces were well adapted to become office suites, and several of the two-story rooms were subdivided to create additional floor space. The architect was Peterson & Brickbauer.

The Art Deco lights from 1931 remained, but in the age before eBay, the furniture, ceremonial garb, objects, and banners were sold to antiques dealers.

UNITED FOREVER

Camp Lockwood,
Defences of Maryland
Hights, Aug 14th/63,
To Corinthian Lodge,
Dear Brothers,

having entered the
Army of the United States,
and being called from the City to
a distant feild of labour, and it
being imposible for me to attend
to the duteis of the education
Committee, I herewith tender to your
honourable body my resignation,
hoping the same may be excepted,
I remain
Yours &c.
In Friendship, Love & Truth,
Charles G. Saunders,

J. MAGEE, 316 Chestnut St., Phila.

CATHEDRAL PLACE

Saratoga and Cathedral Streets
in the heart of downtown Baltimore

An exciting new concept
in office environment

CHARLES T. SISCO.   J. EDWARD SISCO.

SISCO BROS.
MANUFACTURERS & DEALERS IN
Fringes, Gimps, &c.
ODD-FELLOWS' AND MASONIC
REGALIA,
BANNERS, FLAGS,
Military Goods,
SHIPS' SIGNALS, &c.

LADIES' DRESS TRIMMINGS AND VARIETY GOODS.

Baltimore, Sept 20 1865

M Corinthian Lodge No 10 I O O F.

Bought of SISCO BROTHERS,

No. 95 BALTIMORE STREET, opposite Holliday.

6	Velvet Collars & Apron			115 00
1	Marshals Sash			10 00
2	Myrtle Sashs "Guardian"			
8	Birges	1 25		7 50
8	Rosette for Sashes			10 00
1	Baton	65		5 20
13	Lg Dyne Aprons			2 00
1	Marshal Badge			8 00
			1 00	158 70

Recd Paymt
J Sisco Bro

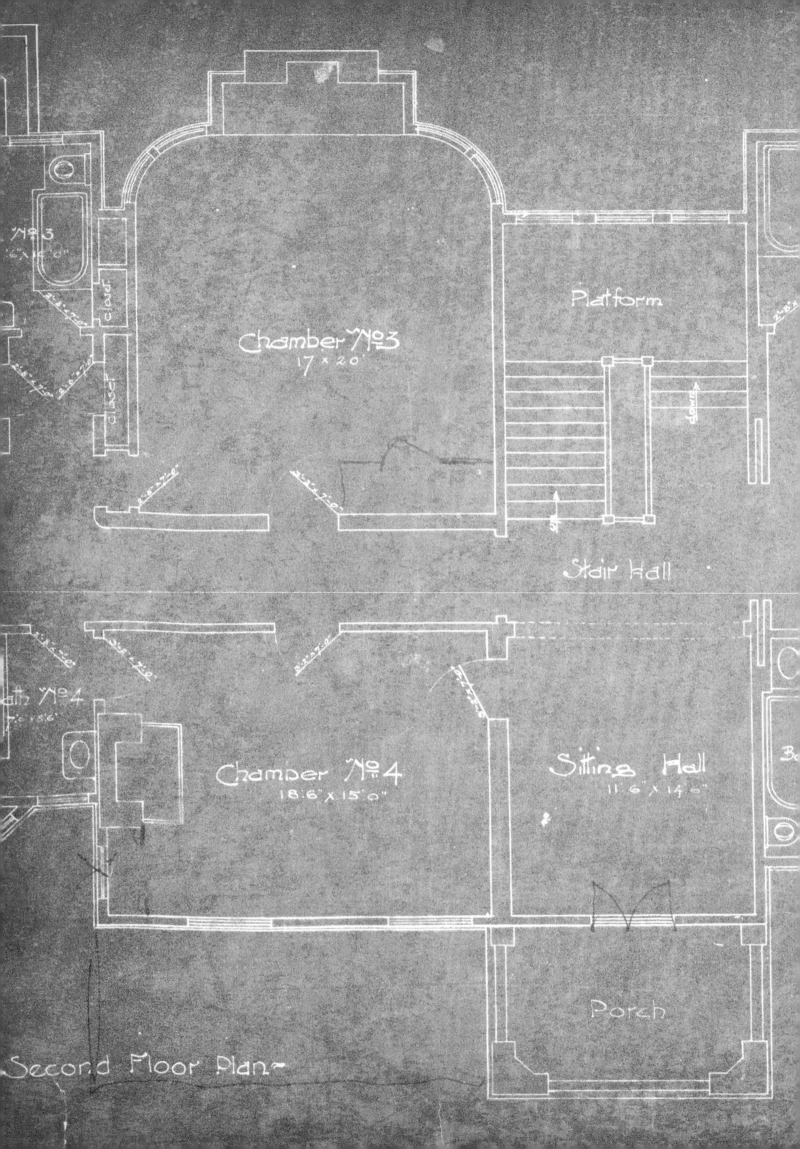

At the beginning of the twentieth century, Baltimore's continuing economic expansion created a huge demand for new types of buildings, especially the office building built of steel with new technological advances like the elevator. The city's seeming unstoppable growth was halted by a catastrophe, the Great Fire of 1904. Over 1,500 buildings in a 140-acre area were destroyed. Baltimore businessmen were undeterred and quickly rebuilt the

1900-PRESENT:
A BOOMING AMERICAN CITY

"Burnt District," continuing the use of historicist architectural styles, especially the Beaux-Arts. While the rebuilding was going on, the industrial expansion surged on with more factories, breweries, and warehouses built around the harbor. The electric streetcar was a catalyst in the growth of Baltimore, as in all American cities, creating a great suburban expansion and allowing workers to commute to their jobs by rapid transit. Baltimore's economy was greatly accelerated by two world wars when Europe entered the conflicts in 1914 and again in 1939. America's entry into the Second World War brought even more industrial growth to the city and Baltimore continued to prosper in the post-war era. Its suburban and economic expansion continued with the population reaching its peak of 949,000 in 1950. But Baltimore went into decline, as did many other American cities, and by 1970, the population had dropped to 905,000. The city had recognized the decline in the late 1950s, and with the aid of the Baltimore business community developed the innovative Urban Renewal Plan, Charles Center, with its first phase completed by the mid-1960s. The city that started out as a single wharf began a road to recovery.

HOTEL JUNKER

HOTEL JUNKER

When people think of raging, out-of-control fires, images of wildfires in California on CNN come immediately to mind. The fire in the fall of 2017 in Santa Rosa, California, destroyed thousands of homes in suburban developments. Awoken in the middle of the night, homeowners had just minutes to escape with their lives. When they returned to the homes several days later, everything they had was gone. Out-of-control fires mainly happen in rural areas today, but at one time they were common events in cities. The Great Chicago Fire of 1871 is probably the most famous.

The Great Baltimore Fire happened in 1904, wiping out 140 acres in 30 hours from February 7 to 8. Starting out as a tiny spark in a pile of wood shavings in the dry-goods store of John E. Hurst on the corner of Liberty Street and what is now Redwood Street, the fire devastated Baltimore's downtown from Fayette Street all the way to the edge of the harbor and the Jones Falls. While the fire was being fought at the John E. Hurst & Company building, a draft of air shot up an elevator shaft, igniting combustible gases and causing an incredibly loud explosion. As a result, the fire spread. From the photos taken of the resulting damage, it looked like an atomic bomb had exploded in the business district. When the fires finally cooled, 1,500 buildings housing 2,500 businesses had been destroyed. More than 35,000 people were out of work because they no longer had any workplaces. But the city was lucky that it happened on a Sunday morning, when everyone was at home or at church. The fire would have been even more destructive if the wind hadn't shifted to the southeast. The new courthouse on the north side of Fayette at Calvert Street just missed being destroyed; the fire miraculously stayed on the south side of Fayette. But two blocks to the west, the fire leapt to the north side of the street, consuming the well-known Hotel Junker.

Downtown hotels in Baltimore and other American cities were quite different from the ones that exist today. Instead of tourists, hotels housed mainly "business travelers," men who represented their companies as wholesalers or "drummers," seeking out business opportunities and making sales. The Hotel Junker, the Carrollton Hotel, and Maltby House were some of the prominent hotels that were destroyed in the fire.

PROPERTY OVERVIEW

Property Name: Hotel Junker

Address: 22 E. Fayette Street, Baltimore, Maryland 21202

Date Built: 1905

Date Restored: 1988

Architectural Style: Beaux-Arts

Original Architect: Charles E. Cassell

Original Use: Fireproof Hotel

Current Use: Offices

Developer: Azola Development Corp.

Contractor: M. P. Azola & Associates, Inc.

Architect: Atelier Three Architects— Werner Mueller & Myrna Poirier

Historic Designation: Contributing Resource, Business and Government Center Historic District, National Register of Historic Places

The Great Baltimore Fire of 1904

Rendering for the 1988 restoration

Intricate stone decoration, restored

The area of destruction was called the "Burnt District." With great public and civic zeal, Baltimore dove into the process of rebuilding literally the week following the fire. It was seen as an opportunity to produce a modern and, most important, fireproof city center. The Baltimore Chapter of the American Institute of Architects called for competitions to redesign the district following the City Beautiful Movement, which was a style of urban design based on grand avenues and parks. The city's business leaders had other ideas, however: they wanted to construct new buildings or repair fire damage as soon as possible—and also get their businesses back as soon as possible. There was no overall design plan for the 140 acres; each owner was on his own. They immediately ordered new plans from architects for their replacement buildings on the existing lots.

Frank Junker hired Charles E. Cassell & Son to design a brand-new 66-room, 7-story hotel, two stories higher than the first. He wanted the $125,000 hotel opened by the summer of 1905 and would personally superintend the construction to make sure the deadline was met. As early as February 24, 1904, members of the American Society of Civil Engineers visited the district for an assessment of

the fire damage. Back in 1799, Baltimore officials knew that combustible construction was a severe fire threat, and had mandated all downtown buildings be built of brick. Still, fires had wiped out smaller sections of the city. The engineers recommended that buildings have wired glass, metal sash, and fireproof shutters on lot lines. Brick and structural clay that had been used in some buildings, particularly as floor fireproofing in steel-framed structures, fared well in the fire. Cassell encased all the hotel's steel structure in concrete and used metal sash. The first floor had a dining room and lobby all clad with green marble, a mahogany bar that H. L. Mencken was said to frequent, and mosaic tile on the first-level concrete floor. Today nearly all hotel rooms have private bathrooms, but like most hotels of the period, the Hotel Junker had only three suites per floor with their own bathrooms, although every room had a sink. Junker improved his new building by installing telephone service in 30 of the rooms. Another fire-prevention innovation was a six-inch pipe from the street running up to the roof; the fire department could use the pipe to connect to a fire hose. Today this is called a standpipe.

The Hotel Junker decayed through the years, as did most downtown buildings housing restaurants, including Cork & Bottle and Humperdinker's. When the hotel was purchased in 1987, it was run-down, especially on the upper floors. The cleanup alone cost $100,000. The building was renovated for office tenants with a unique incentive. Tenants were able to gain a share of real estate ownership based on a one-for-two formula—if you rented 10 percent of the building for five years, you became a 5 percent owner. That left 50 percent ownership for the original development team. Called a tenant equity program, it proved to be an effective incentive, and the building quickly leased up.

The building was gutted, with the interior redesigned by Atelier Three Architects. New HVAC, electrical, and plumbing systems; a new elevator; and all new finishes were included. Cassell's fireproof steel stairs were reused, as well as the marble wainscoting and door trim in some hallways. The limestone exterior, storefronts, and sculptures facing Fayette Street were restored.

The building renovation included one more fireproofing component that Frank Junker and Baltimore City would have appreciated—a fully automatic sprinkler system. If building code had required them, there would never have been a Great Fire.

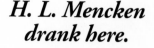

H. L. Mencken drank here.

Newspaper reporters in the old days had a reputation for holding their liquor, and they proved this daily in Baltimore saloons and eateries. H. L. Mencken, the famous literary critic and a reporter for the *Baltimore Sun* and *Morning Herald*, had his favorite watering holes, Marconi's and Schellhase's in particular. And it was said he frequented the bar in the Hotel Junker. He'd been drinking into the wee hours on the morning of the Great Fire and had to roll out of bed to direct the fire's coverage for the *Herald*, staying up for the next 64 hours.

Hotel Junker building to get new life

Tenants offered ownership shares

By Edward Gunts

The Hotel Junker, once one of Baltimore's most distinctive small hotels, now sits vacant and unused on East Fayette Street, one of many downtown buildings that seem to have been overlooked during Baltimore's renaissance.

But a Baltimore County-based developer believes he may have found a way to bring the 82-year-old hotel, and other old buildings like it, back into productive service.

Martin P. Azola, president of M. P. Azola Inc., recently contracted to purchase the seven-story building at 22 E. Fayette St., and plans to convert it into office space for small professional firms. Construction will begin this spring.

The unusual aspect of the project is that the developer is providing an incentive for prospective tenants by offering them a share of ownership in the building in return for leasing space for at least five years.

Under the developer's "tenant-equity" program, tenants automatically become limited partners in the project, explained Nancy Roberts, a real estate development officer for Azola.

"What we're doing is offering tenants, on a one-for-two basis, equity pro-rated to the space they take in the building," she said. "If they take space equivalent to 10 percent of the building, they will automatically get

See **JUNKER**, 14G, Col. 3

Architect' rendering of 22 East Fayette St

Hotel Junker

Stag   European Plan

Absolutely Fire Proof

FRANK JUNKER, Prop.

Telephone Connections in Every Room

20 and 22 E. FAYETTE STREET

Near Charles Street

BALTIMORE, MD.

BROMO-SELTZER TOWER

Seattle has the Space Needle, Paris its Eiffel Tower, and Baltimore has the distinctive Emerson Bromo-Seltzer Tower. Cities have skylines with towering skyscrapers, but often it is an eccentric structure that its inhabitants come to love most. Baltimore's beloved icon has its roots in a headache remedy that is still used today. Isaac Emerson, a chemist trained at the University of North Carolina, moved to Baltimore in 1880 and opened a drugstore. He later patented a formula for an antacid called Bromo-Seltzer and in 1887 created the Emerson Drug Company to produce it. Captain (he was active in the Maryland Naval Reserves) Emerson understood the importance of marketing and developed one of the first comprehensive advertising campaigns in the late-nineteenth century to promote his product. Bromo-Seltzer became world famous, especially in combating hangovers, and Emerson became enormously wealthy.

Emerson wanted his product to advertise itself just by its appearance alone, so he bottled Bromo-Seltzer's white granules in a distinctive cobalt-blue glass bottle. The color and shape of the bottle became instantly recognizable. With his great success came the need for larger production facilities, and in 1911 Emerson built a new factory at the corner of West Lombard and South Eutaw Streets in downtown Baltimore. But its design was unlike that of any other American factory of its day. Like most men of great wealth, Emerson had taken a grand tour of Europe and was much impressed with the Palazzo Vecchio, a 308-foot-tall thirteenth-century stone watchtower in Florence. When his architect, Joseph Evans Sperry, began to design the new facility, Emerson instructed him to use the Palazzo as inspiration. The six-story factory was connected to a 288-foot-high tower with battlements and detailing very much like the original Palazzo. In its makeover for business, the 15-story tower was framed with steel and faced with ocher brick that housed

PROPERTY OVERVIEW

Property Name: Emerson Bromo-Seltzer Tower

Address: 21 South Eutaw Street, Baltimore, Maryland 21201

Date Built: 1911

Date Restored: 2007 & 2017

Architectural Style: Romanesque Revival

Original Architect: Joseph Evans Sperry

Original Use: Vertical Circulation, Emerson Drug Company Factory

Current Use: Artist Studios

Developer: Baltimore Office of Promotion and the Arts (Bill Gilmore) with Eddie C. & C. Sylvia Brown

Contractor: Azola & Associates, Inc. & Azola Building Rehab, Inc.

Clock Restoration: Balzer Family Clock Works

Architect: SMG Architects (2007 rehab)

Engineer: Skarda & Associates, Inc.

Historic Designation: Baltimore City Landmark and National Register of Historic Places

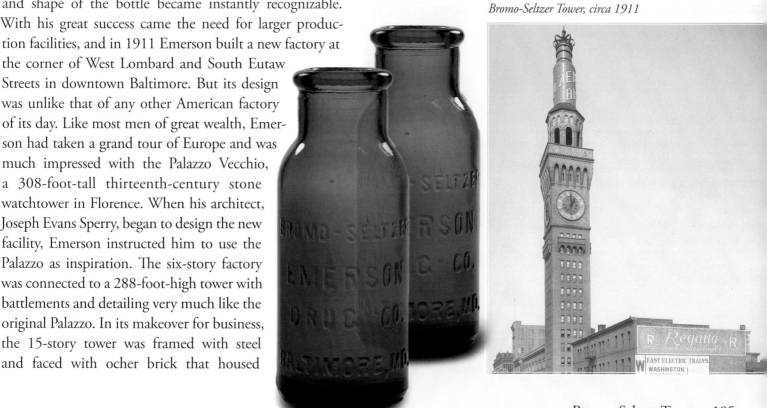

Bromo-Seltzer Tower, circa 1911

Before there were drones, there were human flies.

Today a drone would be sent up buzzing from side to side of the tower, sending images to a laptop showing every square inch of the tower's surface. Previously, humans were sent to do the condition survey. Rappelling down the sides of the tower and crawling over its walls like human flies 200 feet above the street, the survey team was only protected by rope harnesses (and nerves of steel).

executive offices. On its four sides were clock faces bigger than England's Big Ben. The 12 letters in Bromo-Seltzer worked perfectly as numerals.

But Emerson, a genius in advertising, was not finished. Atop the tower was placed a 17-ton, 51-foot-high revolving blue Bromo bottle with 596 lights that could be seen from Maryland's Eastern Shore. The bottle was removed in 1936 because it was believed to be

causing structural damage to the tower. When Emerson Drug Company moved to Pennsylvania, its factory was demolished and replaced with a fire station, but the tower was donated to the city on the condition that it would be saved. It sat vacant for years because the fire marshal would not allow a 15-story building to have only one fire stair.

When the city finally turned its attention to the tower in the 1990s, it created a for-profit public/private partnership

15-story shaft cut for new stair

Clock and glass restoration

with local entrepreneur and philanthropist Eddie C. Brown and his wife, C. Sylvia, to fund its renovation. The concept was to create studio space for artists who would pay rent. The first order of business for the Azola company was to make the tower code compliant with fire-safety regulations, which meant building a second smoke-protected stair within its 900-square-foot footprint. To do this meant cutting through 15 floors of plaster and concrete embedded with an enormous amount of reinforcing bar, which took three months of solid demolition. Because of the tight space constraints, the new stair had to be built in pieces on the ground then hoisted up floor by floor to be welded in place. The original manual elevator was restored and the other elevator was modernized. The addition of the stair left little room for studio space, allowing only three people per floor, but the studio space still rented up. The presence of this artist community was the catalyst for the city to create the Bromo Tower Arts and Entertainment District, anchored by the tower on the south.

With the interior done and the building safe, attention was turned to its famous exterior, which had suffered from neglect for decades. To understand the scope of the work that had to be done, a complete inventory of the tower's exterior condition had to be surveyed by rappelling down its sides. The four elevations were closely studied for signs of decay in the ocher brick, the stone balconies, the terra-cotta, and glazed clock faces. The structural problems were discovered to be caused by a rusting interior steel structure that was expanding against the brick and causing the tower's vertical cracking.

A plan of preservation and repair was developed—the brick piers of the cupola had to be rebuilt, this time with cathodic protection to prevent the expansion of the steel; the concrete spalling at the bottom of the cupola had to be repaired, for fear of pieces falling to the street and killing someone; the ocher brick had to be repointed and cleaned to original color. Work would start on the balconies, which

200-pound clock hand in for repair

had been covered in sheet metal to hold them together. A new flat roof had to be installed on the cupola. In the 1930s, Emerson had installed pieces of steel to try to fix the cracking, and they needed to be removed.

The tower's main feature, the Seth Thomas clock, had been running on electricity for years instead of its original gravity mechanism. The Balzer Family Clock Works of Free-port, Maine, restored the clock and cleaned its giant dial faces. The tower's clock room is a strange sight, with its systems of gears and wheels lit by soft light coming through the obscured glass of the clock faces. The restoration of the balconies, which included removing their non-original metal cladding, was also planned. New LED lights were installed to up-light the cupola in a variety of colors.

The exterior work is an ongoing project, and the Bromo-Seltzer Tower continues to look better and better, truer to its original 1911 condition. But the one item that will not be restored is the giant blue bottle. The steel framework, minus its cobalt-blue glass, was actually found rusting away in a farm field in nearby Anne Arundel County.

Clock ready for another 100 years

The cupola undergoes repair.

New clock works

GREENSPRING MONTESSORI AT EMERSON FARM

PROPERTY OVERVIEW

Property Name: Greenspring Montessori at Emerson Farm

Address: 10807 Tony Drive, Lutherville/Timonium, Maryland 21093

Date Built: 1916

Date Restored: 1976

Architectural Style: Vernacular

Original Architect: Unknown

Original Use: Dairy Barn

Current Use: Montessori School

Developer: Brooklandwood Associates, LP (Joseph Azola)

Contractor: J. R. Azola & Associates, Inc.

Architect: James R. Grieves

Rich Baltimoreans never stayed in the city during the summer. They would go to cool-air vacation spots for the wealthy, like the Poconos in Pennsylvania or the Berkshires in Massachusetts, or they would travel just a few miles north to Baltimore County to their permanent summer homes. Not only was this annual excursion a refreshing respite, it gave rich men the opportunity to play "gentleman farmer," patterned on the British aristocracy's model, which they admired greatly. Captain Isaac Emerson, a chemist who made a fortune from the headache remedy Bromo-Seltzer, fancied himself a dairy farmer. Every year, Emerson would come up from his mansion on Eutaw Place to his Brooklandwood estate, at the intersection of Falls and Greenspring Valley Roads, to tend to his Guernsey herd. There he had built his Brooklandwood dairy complex, complete with reinforced concrete silos, barns, stables, and even a cow exhibition barn.

The land was originally owned by Charles Carroll, a signer of the Declaration of Independence, who built a Federal-style mansion in the mid-1790s that is now part of Saint Paul's School. Emerson was the third owner after George Brown, the son of the founder of Alex. Brown & Sons. In 1916, Emerson built two long one-story barns with rubble stone walls and eyebrow dormers. Emerson would leave another legacy of sorts in Baltimore County: his daughter, Margaret, married Alfred Gwynne Vanderbilt, who died in 1915 in the sinking of the ocean liner RMS *Lusitania* when it was hit by a German torpedo. Emerson's grandson, Alfred Gwynne Vanderbilt II, became a leader in American thoroughbred horse racing and built Sagamore Farm, a famous racing stable nearby in Baltimore County. Vanderbilt would also be the man who leveled Pimlico's

Emerson's old barn, circa 1975

Lady Fifi wouldn't recognize the place.

Captain Isaac Emerson, the trained chemist who invented Bromo-Seltzer, was a gentleman dairy farmer at his estate in Brooklandville. The long stone barns he erected housed his prized Guernsey cows. He loved competing and winning competitions with them and had great affection for his milkers, giving them names like Lady Fifi, Buttermaid, and Hyacinth.

infield, also called Old Hilltop (page 52). When Captain "Ike" died in 1931, his wife, Anne, inherited the property, and then she left it to her daughter, Ethel Looram.

Over the years, Emerson Farm became a popular Sunday driving destination, attracting thousands of visitors to buy the Brooklandwood dairy's milk quarts and home-made ice cream. Starting in 1948, and for the next twenty years, one of the barns was used for summer theater. The land was eventually sold by Emerson's heirs to Joseph Azola for residential development, but in 1976 the Greenspring Montessori School purchased seven acres of that land, including the dairy complex. Based on a design by architect James R. Grieves, the two barns were recycled to create a school. A new infill addition with a main entrance that joined the buildings together was constructed. The barns themselves were solidly built and readily converted into the school. Grieves's sensitive design retained many of the historic elements, including the wide horizontal window openings, the attic lofts and their loading doors, the exposed heavy timber framing, the unique eyebrow dormers, and the metal ventilators along the roof ridges. Windows were installed in the big barn door openings. The two cross dormers, with their original loft doors on the barn, as well as the three big silos with their concave conical metal caps, stayed in place.

Like St. Paul's School nearby, Greenspring Montessori School was now set in a beautiful and tranquil location. The school is still there. In 2017, a $7 million renovation project of the campus was announced; it will also include a new building.

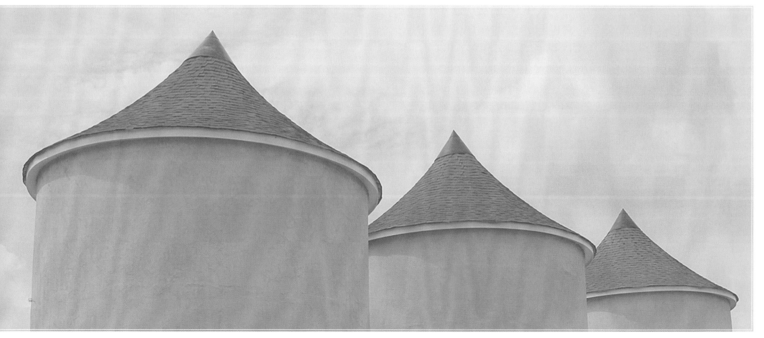

The signature silos

Above: Ready for school Below: An early class, circa 1977

KING SYRUP PLANT

Today everyone wants a view of Baltimore's harbor from their windows and decks. But in Key Highway's industrial heyday, no one cared about the views of the water. When the Mangels-Herold Company built their new plant in 1919 at 1414 Key Highway, at the corner Boyle Street, overlooking the harbor, the only concern was making money from a product they'd invented in 1901—King Syrup. The thick, sweet, dark brown syrup had quickly become a mainstay of Southern cooking—"America's Finest Table Syrup."

Not to be confused with pancake syrup, King Syrup, and its distinctive red label with a lion's head, was a table syrup that could be poured over any kind of food—and it was. Pancakes were smothered in King Syrup as well, and many preferred it over maple syrup. It was used in almost every type of baking recipe—pies, cookies, caramel corn, cakes, and candies. So beloved was the syrup, that it found its way into vegetable dishes, salads, baked beans, breads, and main dishes like roasts and chicken. Shoofly pies in Pennsylvania Dutch cooking were made with nothing else. Some devotees would pour it onto a tablespoon and take it like it was medicine. Mangels-Herold soon started producing cookbooks like *70 Famous King Syrup Recipes*, because the syrup had become so popular. The syrup sponsored a radio show on NBC in the 1940s, with commercials using their catchy "Swing to King" jingle.

The King Syrup plant was well located on Key Highway and received shipments of barrels of molasses and corn syrup from freighters docked just a couple hundred yards away. These sticky ingredients were pumped into a tank on the plant's roof. A companion product that was almost as popular was King Po-T-Rik molasses, which had a stronger taste and darker color and came in a bottle with a blue label. The company expanded their product line in the 1950s, introducing laundry products that included King Liquid Starch and the first fabric softener, King Fluff.

The factories that lined Key Highway, like King Syrup, were once the symbol of Baltimore's manufacturing and industrial might. On both sides of its wide road were factories, shipping facilities, and plants that produced goods from metal fabrication, canneries, locomotive repair, and oil refining. Connected to a waterfront, the businesses

PROPERTY OVERVIEW

Property Name: King Syrup Plant, The Mangels-Herold Co.

Address: 1414 Key Highway, Baltimore, Maryland 21230

Date Built: 1919

Date Restored: 2002–2012

Architectural Style: Twentieth-Century Industrial

Original Architect: Unknown

Original Use: Manufacturing Plant for King Syrup Products

Current Use: Offices and Retail

Developer: 1414 Key Highway Holdings, LLC (Azola Family and others)

Contractor: Azola & Associates, Inc.

Architect: Marks Thomas Architects

Product rolls off the line, circa 1940.

Contemporary offices overlook the harbor.

The plant spans four buildings, covering a city block.

BDC: 'Polish, not demolish'

BY RACHEL MANSOUR
Daily Record Business Writer

The Baltimore Development Corp. is betting the South Harbor Business Center, a four-building light industrial and office campus in South Baltimore that it has owned for more than five years, has value in its current state.

That's why it selected, over two other proposals, a development team's $6 million plan to "polish, not demolish," the nearly 80,000-square-foot complex, officials said yesterday.

The SHBC Partnership, a joint venture of Azola Associates Inc., Banks Contracting Co. Inc. and The Morris Weinman Co., will acquire the 1.2-acre parcel at 1414 Key Highway, historically rehabilitate two buildings, create 35 basement

parking spaces in one building and complete minor improvements to the two warehouse structures.

Since the complex is 70 percent occupied with 11 tenants, including the Greater Baltimore Technology Development Center, an incubator for start-up companies, the developers will either renovate interior portions of the property after leases expire, by 2003 or 2004, or fix up spaces if tenants comply.

The team has worked together on five other Baltimore rehabilitation projects.

Its plan was chosen over A&R Development Corp.'s proposal to create 45,000 square feet of Class B office and retail space, eliminating industrial uses and Struever Bros.

SEE SOUTH HARBOR PAGE 8A

had access to raw materials and to shipping for exporting products. The proximity to the waterfront also provided a ready source for working-class labor in the surrounding South Baltimore neighborhoods. The 1920s was an era of great industrial expansion in the city, producing major businesses such as Proctor & Gamble and the Domino Sugar refining plant. But by the 1950s, manufacturing was on the wane due to outdated railroad facilities, decreased investment, and competition from surrounding ports. The death knell came in 1983 when Bethlehem Steel's Key Highway shipyard was sold to developers to turn the properties into high-rise apartments.

In 1992, the Baltimore City Planning Department approved both the Key Highway Urban Renewal Plan, which encouraged residential areas, and the Key Highway East Industrial Area Urban Renewal Plan, aimed at protecting existing industries and discouraging speculation on the land between Harbor View and the Domino Sugar plant. Another plan in 2004 tried to balance residential and

industrial development, but it was never implemented. In 2004 the housing boom and another effort, the Key Highway Urban Renewal Plan amendment, helped put into effect some of the recommendations of the 1992 study. Property was rezoned, and steps were taken to make sure views of the harbor weren't cut off by new residential development. But the issue of the underused waterfront wasn't resolved.

The King Syrup plant, which had grown to a complex of four interconnected buildings, was closed in 1985 and sold to Baltimore City. The reinforced concrete-frame buildings with brick infill and steel industrial sash windows were leased out as a small-business incubator by the Baltimore Development Corporation (BDC) over a period of 15 years. Then, in 2001, the Azola family was the operating member of the team who had a plan to rehab the properties while also emphasizing the historic preservation of the plant. New, historically compatible and energy-efficient windows were installed, the concrete

structural frames and brick walls were repaired, and new corridors and flexible office spaces were created.

At the same time the rehab was under way, the architectural firm of Marks Thomas was looking to relocate from the Old Goucher district, and they approached the developer about the building. The only space left was the plant's dank, inhospitable, street-level truck terminal, but the architects used their creativity to transform the space into studio spaces and offices. Other tenants included Race Pace Bikes, Home on the Harbor Furniture, the *Daily Record*, Better Business Bureau, and Marinalife.

King Syrup has since been sold to Carriage House Brands, which continues to make the syrup that's poured on pancakes and biscuits throughout America. But it hasn't been forgotten in its old home at 1414 Key Highway: one of the tenants, an advertising firm called Planit, incorporated the famous red label into a mural on its office wall.

PARCEL POST STATION

1501   Saint Paul

RAILWAY   EXPRESS

RAILWAY EXPRESS BUILDING

Today, Americans take it for granted that they can take a package to be mailed to their local post office. But parcel postal service wasn't adopted by the U.S. Post Office until 1913. So up until then, private companies like Adams Express or Wells Fargo delivered parcels. Americans, especially those in the countryside, demanded that the U.S. Post Office deliver parcels because the private companies charged too much or didn't bother with unprofitable rural routes. After 1913, Americans could send parcels at a modest cost. Today, with online shopping, private companies like FedEx and UPS again dominate parcel shipping.

In 1928, a new main post office was to be built in downtown Baltimore, with a parcel post station on a separate site to be determined. The building of the station would be done through a relatively sophisticated development process for the time. It would be built and paid for by a private developer who would lease the building to the U.S. Post Office. The Indianapolis developer who was awarded the project used a novel (by Baltimore standards) New York City real estate device—air rights. The developer secured a lease with the Pennsylvania Railroad to build above a piece of its land between the Jones Falls and the Penn Station tracks. The new parcel post station was built on concrete piers or "stilts" 25 feet high so its first floor aligned with St. Paul Street. Beneath the station were four tracks with platforms so mail cars could load and unload packages. Freight elevators ran down to the tracks to take packages back up to the station. At the time of the station's construction, railroads carried the bulk of America's mail, but this would change over the coming decades as trucks began supplanting the railroad. The U.S. Post Office anticipated this by creating a driveway connecting St. Paul and Calvert Streets. Airmail service had also become a method of transport, its popularity spurred by Charles Lindbergh's famous transatlantic flight in 1927. The medallion on the front facade of the station has a trimotor plane very similar to Lindbergh's *Spirit of St. Louis.* In the station's first year of service in 1930, it handled 31 million parcels.

PROPERTY OVERVIEW

Property Name: Railway Express Building

Address: 1501 St. Paul Street, Baltimore, Maryland 21202

Date Built: 1929

Date Restored: 2007

Architectural Style: Neoclassical

Original Use: Post Office

Current Use: Offices and Apartments

Developer: Railway Express, LLC (Azola Family and others)

Contractor: Doracon, Azola & Associates, Inc.

Architect: Hord Coplan Macht

Engineer: Morabito Consultants

Awards: Preservation Award—Baltimore Heritage, 2008

Historic Designation: National Register of Historic Places

Air rights building on columns, 25 feet above the train tracks

When a new central post office that also handled parcel post mail was built in 1973, the U.S. Post Office sold the building to the City of Baltimore, which used it as its rehab services center for the Housing Authority until 2002, when they sold it to a development group. The building was always mistakenly called the Railway Express Building, largely because there had been a 30-foot-long sign for that company along the driveway (which was eventually demolished to build the Penn Station parking garage).

The Parcel Post Station was listed on the National Register of Historic Places, so historic tax credits for the project could be used to fund its adaptive reuse into a commercial-residential complex called Railway Express Lofts. That meant most of the exterior and interior features had to be retained in the new design. Throughout its history, the U.S. Post Office built facilities meant to last, by using high-quality materials and a high standard of design quality. The 85,000-square-foot station, essentially a warehouse used to process parcel post mail, was a monumental and imposing Classical Revival style built of reinforced concrete with an exterior of limestone, buff brick, and terra-cotta trim. Its ornate entry, tall steel windows, American eagle medallions and spandrel panels on four elevations were all intact, making the exterior easy to retain. The high-ceilinged, open-space interior gave the project architects, Hord Coplan Macht, the flexibility to design modernist-style apartments with tiered spaces. A typical apartment would have a combination living-room-dining-room-kitchen space lit by a huge window. Then behind that space would be a stair leading to the upper-level bedrooms, with large interior windows to let daylight in. Bright accent colors were painted on walls, and wall sconces bounced light off the tall ceilings. In some of the apartments, one could look up and see sections of the old surveillance catwalks, which were the most prominent historic features on the interior and had to be kept. The street-level loading dock on the north side of the building was also retained; its wide openings were converted into storefronts.

While Azola's construction of the interior of the building went smoothly, there were great challenges to overcome outside its footprint. The waterline, which ran from Mt. Royal Avenue to under the Calvert Street bridge (now called the Duke Ellington Bridge) and then over the Jones Falls Expressway, froze and ruptured during the winter and needed to be completely replaced. It was discovered that there was no gas service in the building, so it had to be redesigned for electric heating. But then Baltimore Gas and Electric said the incoming power feed was insufficient, so a brand-new primary electrical service had to also be run (and be paid for by the developer) under the bridge, over the expressway.

But in the end, the project was amazingly completed in just ten months, and then fully leased up within six months. Many people who lived in Baltimore and worked in Washington, DC, found it convenient to just walk across the street to Penn Station to catch their trains. As the district's first major project, Railway Express Lofts was in the vanguard of the redevelopment of the Station North Arts and Entertainment District. Today the area is thriving.

Monumental facade viewed from Penn Station.

Don't steal any mail – you're being watched!

The rate of theft by employees in the U.S. Post Office was so high that surveillance catwalks had to be installed in their facilities across the nation. Crisscrossing the ceilings in the Railway Express Building were completely plaster-enclosed catwalks, each accessed by an enclosed spiral stair. Postal inspectors would walk along and look through peepholes in the catwalk walls and floors to see if employees were stealing or tampering with parcels. Until the advent of closed-circuit video cameras in the 1980s, most large postal facilities had surveillance catwalks.

VOLUNTEERS OF AMERICA

Most of the time, an old building that's recycled into a new use is a fine old historic structure, an exemplar of a particular architectural style from the nineteenth or early twentieth century. Many industrial buildings, like breweries, warehouses, and factories that produced every sort of product from that period, have become new homes for businesses or apartments. The common denominator in all these buildings is that the owners insisted that these utilitarian buildings possess some architectural quality, be it fancy brickwork or great arched windows and entries. But after World War II, companies discovered steel kit-built structures in which to store or manufacture their goods. They consisted of a steel arched frame sheathed in corrugated sheet metal, with a few windows at the entry. The handsome brick-and-stone industrial buildings became a thing of the past. Prefab steel buildings were modular in design and less expensive to build. These utilitarian, metal buildings multiplied across the American landscape, especially in a new urban development concept of the postwar era called the industrial park. Just one building could cover several acres of land. With high ceilings, concrete slab floors, fluorescent lighting, and bays of garage doors, they were perfect industrial homes.

The Durrett Sheppard Steel Company's warehouse at 4900 East Monument Street was exactly that kind of building. Built in 1965, it covered 52,000 square feet, on three and a half acres of land, to house the company's finished metal products with its own railroad access dock. But as companies evolve, they sell off unneeded space, so in 2012 the vast warehouse was up for sale. The Volunteers of America (VOA) Chesapeake, which provides facilities to help newly released prisoners make the transition back into the community, was looking for a new home. They had outgrown the nearby run-down motel they were using. Accepting offenders who are transferred from a federal prison for prerelease programming, under the supervision of the U.S. Probation and Pretrial Services System, VOA helps them by providing employment assistance and

PROPERTY OVERVIEW

Property Name: Volunteers of America

Original Address: 4900 E. Monument Street, Baltimore, Maryland 21205

Date Built: 1965

Date Restored: 2013

Architectural Style: Warehouse

Original Use: Steel Fabrication, Durrett Sheppard Steel Company

Current Use: Residential Re-Entry Center

Developer: Volunteers of America Chesapeake

Architect: Marks Thomas Architects

Contractor: Azola Building Rehab, Inc.

Engineer: Skarda & Associates, Inc.

Original rear railroad access

A salvaged building that helps people salvage their lives.

When prisoners finish their sentences, they want to make a new start in life — to salvage their lives—but they face enormous obstacles. No one usually wants to hire or give an ex-convict a second chance. VOA has helped thousands of men and women make that difficult transition.

placement, educational and vocational training, substance abuse education, and life skills to make that successful transition. The huge empty building was purchased and the design and construction of a new state-of-the-art residential re-entry center began.

Designed by Marks Thomas Architects, the metal-clad warehouse was transformed by the Azola company into a 148-bed facility, with each dorm room housing five to ten residents. A computer lab, staff offices, a dining room, media classrooms, TV lounges, and an indoor basketball court were also created. Because of the 35-foot-high ceilings, a 25,000 square-foot second level was built over the new spaces for future expansion. The four giant 10-ton, overhead cranes Durrett Sheppard used for moving steel were left behind and later incorporated into the design of the common spaces, thus retaining the original industrial use of the building.

The practical steel building is still industrial-looking on the outside, but with imaginative design, its interior is a welcoming home to men and women facing a daunting challenge—to once more lead a normal life.

The original 10-ton overhead cranes used for moving steel were incorporated into the design.

MERCANTILE SAFE DEPOSIT AND TRUST COMPANY BUILDING

"The most admirable of the commercial buildings in Baltimore." This was a compliment, paid by architecture critic Montgomery Schuyler in his essay, "The Romanesque Revival in America," to the 1886 Mercantile Safe Deposit and Trust Company Building at Redwood and Calvert Streets. It could just as well apply to the bank's new headquarters, built at 2 Hopkins Plaza in 1969 and supervised by Joseph Azola. The 24-story reinforced concrete building was constructed as part of Baltimore's Charles Center project, a major urban redevelopment plan created to revive a section of the city's downtown that was in decline. It was a private-sector initiative in partnership with the government to link the retail district on the west to the government district in the east. When the plan was developed in 1958, modernist architecture was at it apogee, which meant there was little regard for the historic architecture of the nineteenth and early twentieth centuries that existed in the 33-acre Charles Center site. Many buildings were bulldozed to make way for modernist architecture in a mixed-use plan that combined government and private office space, underground parking, retail, housing, restaurants, and the Morris A. Mechanic Theatre. The project was built in about 15 years and was hailed as a national example of urban redevelopment. When Charles Center was complete in 1975, the Inner Harbor project was next in line.

In the 43 years since it was completed, people have had mixed feelings about the success of Charles Center. Some say it was a failure that destroyed the downtown and did little for the city's revitalization. Along with many historic buildings that were swept away, the project was wrong to abandon traditional street patterns. It was an example of modernist architects' arrogant belief in the power of modern architecture—that it could transform cities—and it showed their complete disdain for the past.

The Original Mercantile building at Redwood and Calvert Streets

No matter what one's views are of the project's legacy, it produced some outstanding modernist buildings, beginning with Ludwig Mies van der Rohe's One Charles Center of 1959, which set the standard for future architectural design in Charles Center. A key concept in the Charles Center planning was the inclusion of high architectural quality in commercial buildings. The new Mercantile Safe Deposit and Trust Company Building was another celebrated architectural design. Designed by the firm most people consider Baltimore's best modernist firm of the period, Peterson & Brickbauer, Mercantile was created using modern materials, such as reinforced concrete, in new ways. It was essentially a speculative office building, and its developer had to find a major tenant because it was a key requirement for financing the project. The bank became the lead tenant, thus giving its name to the building. Since the late-nineteenth century, banks grew from stand-alone buildings to just one of many tenants in a multistory office building. Moving from its old two-story building at Calvert and Redwood Streets, Mercantile placed their bank offices on the lower eight floors, while the upper floors were rented to lawyers, architects, businesses, and accountants. In addition to the tower, a reinforced concrete-and-glass pavilion was built to the south. Originally, Mercantile was going to use the pavilion as the public banking hall but instead switched it to the first floor of the tower. As with the rest of Charles Center, retail and restaurants never succeeded in the tower's base. Below the building were two floors of parking and one floor to house the bank's vaults.

"The structure of the building is the architecture of the building," said Peterson & Brickbauer. The tower's concrete load-bearing exterior columns, which gave the building a commanding verticality, were divided into seven bays across its north and south facades. Between the columns were wide windows that were in turn divided by vertical stainless-steel tracks used for window washing, a clever way of combining practicality with design detailing. The square pavilion sharing the plaza to the south is a jewel-box design of a reinforced concrete structure enclosed on all sides by a two-story glass window wall. Four great pyramidal skylights bring natural light into the space. Peterson & Brickbauer would go on to design other highly admired office buildings in the Charles Center project.

As American cities like Baltimore evolved, the original uses of its buildings changed as well. Factories that once produced cigars, furniture, or cardboard boxes; warehouses that contained goods; and even churches were converted into other types of buildings, mainly apartments, which have brought people back into the city. Some of the great office buildings built in downtown Baltimore in the late-nineteenth and early-twentieth centuries now house apartment dwellers instead of office workers. And today, modernist office buildings are being converted into residential buildings. The Mercantile tower is well suited for such a conversion and is in the process of becoming an apartment building. This change dovetails with its history. It was built in the 1960s as part of the Charles Center project, whose goal was to rejuvenate Baltimore. Now the Mercantile Safe Deposit and Trust Building is part of a new phase to bring life back into the city.

"I consider this to be among the best we produced. It has the most straight-forward expression of Gothic clarity. The structure is the architecture, and the architecture is the structure. Exposed concrete was the real challenge....Fifty years later, the concrete looks the same as when it was finished."

Charles Brickbauer, Architect

Alpha and Omega

Imagine building a new structure and having it listed on the National Register of Historic Places 50 years later.

British American Properties, Ltd. developed the Mercantile Safe Deposit and Trust Company Building and the adjacent two-story pavilion in 1969. Joseph R. Azola was their U.S. representative for the entire project.

With 50 years as the benchmark for placing buildings on the National Register of Historic Places, many post–World War II buildings across America are being designated as eminent examples of modernist design, including some of the buildings constructed in Charles Center. Now the Peterson & Brickbauer and Azola family legacies have been greatly enhanced: the Mercantile Safe Deposit and Trust Company Building has been nominated for inclusion on the National Register.

THE AZOLA FAMILY

A BUILDING LEGACY

Written by Martin P. Azola

Old buildings decay and die unless given new uses. The Azola family has been working together for more than 50 years in Baltimore, finding and repurposing many significant historic buildings. What a wonderful way to make a living . . . breathing new life into historic structures . . . giving them another shot at usefulness.

Here is my recollection of our family history:

Pietro Azzoli immigrates to America.

A mason from Monte Casino, Italy, Grandpa Pete (Pietro Azzoli) came to America during the wave of early twentieth-century immigration. He first worked in the concrete trades, building dams on the Mississippi River—they used to say he could lift two 90-pound bags of cement under each arm, and throw them into the mixer.

Naturalized in 1944 as Peter Azola, he moved to Detroit, Michigan, where he continued to work in the trades, and where he finished out his years. Grandpa and Grandma Christina had two children, Joseph and Lucy Azola.

Joseph R. Azola continues the family "building" legacy.

Joseph (Dad) worked side by side with Grandpa Pete until the outbreak of World War II. He was making a whopping $119.70 a month when honorably discharged from the Marines, where he had been a rifle sharpshooter and combat photographer. He then attended the Illinois Institute of Technology at night, studying drafting.

Dad married Lillian A. Zeeman from Chicago, Illinois, in 1945. Lillian's father, Martin Zeeman, had been an engineer for the Santa Fe Railroad, while mother Alice

ran the household. Joe and Lillian (Lynn) had two children, Martin (that's me) and my brother, Stephen. Steve elected to make his mark in the concours quality classic automobile restoration field, and producing custom bass guitars. He lives in Escondido, California.

Lillian Azola as a young woman, now celebrating 98 years.

Pietro Azzoli (Peter Azola), 1892–1967

After the war, Dad started his own business, the J. R. Azola Construction Company, in the vibrant city of Detroit. The business quickly became a successful heavy-construction company, building treatment plants, roads, and buildings. I remember seeing a new Chrysler sitting in the driveway every year, straight from the Detroit Auto Show.

Then, unexpectedly, his company, with us in tow, moved to Phoenix, Arizona, with a new name—the Euclid Construction Company. Euclid constructed a causeway from the Colorado River, bringing much-needed irrigation to the Parker, Arizona, region. During that time, Dad became the sheriff of Parker (with a population of 1,201 and an average July temperature of 108 degrees).

Dad never told me the details, but Euclid closed after just one year. He took a job with Tippets-Abbet-McCarthy-Stratton, a large international engineering company, building grain silos for Iraq's Prince Faisal in Baghdad and Basra. In 1958 there were numerous coups d'état in the region, and it was a race for Westerners to get out of the country amid the riots and chaos. We came back to the States and settled in Chicago with my maternal grandparents, for a time.

Then one day Dad announced that we were moving to Baltimore, Maryland. It was portrayed as a beautiful city on the Atlantic Ocean. But, actually, the family landed in Towson. He was to be the chief engineer for the construction of a new town called Joppatowne. So, in 1966, Joseph Azola opened his own business at 305 West Chesapeake Avenue in Towson—J. R. Azola & Associates, Inc. His most noteworthy project was the overseeing of the construction of the 24-story Mercantile Safe Deposit and Trust Building located at 2 Hopkins Plaza, in downtown Baltimore.

Before long, he was assembling a portfolio of historic buildings to redevelop for the bank chairman's trust. That portfolio grew to dozens of buildings, with over 500,000 square feet of space. His firm developed, coordinated design, rehabbed, and managed the properties throughout the 1970s. They were all located in Baltimore City.

Dad's final focus took a change in direction with an opportunity to develop 100 acres of land in Baltimore County. He envisioned a clustered community of town houses on 30 acres of ground, surrounded by 40 acres of open space, designed to entice affluent purchasers. And so began the Rockland experience, which also included the restoration of the Rockland Grist Mill and the construction of the Risteau with luxury condominium residences.

Joseph R. Azola died unexpectedly in 1982, before all of Rockland had been completed, leaving me to carry on . . . the third generation of Azolas . . . just as passionate about rebuilding and repurposing many of Baltimore's historic buildings as my father.

Martin P. Azola carries on the legacy.

I was the first college graduate in the Azola family, and pursued degrees in civil engineering at Virginia Polytechnic Institute (now Virginia Tech), and was commissioned as an officer in the Air Force immediately following graduation.

I married my lovely high school sweetheart, the former Lone Tidemand of Copenhagen, Denmark, 50 years ago. After we said our "I do's," we were stationed for four years in Alaska, where I was an engineer in the 5010th Combat Support Group, Alaskan Air Command. We then came back home to Baltimore to join my dad's business and start our family. We were blessed with three beautiful children, Anthony, Matthew, and Kirsten.

After Dad's untimely death, I dove back into the business of rehabilitation and interior improvement for many of Baltimore's downtown historic buildings and M. P. Azola & Associates, Inc. ultimately grew to more than 250 employees. We branched out into historic building and land development starting with Rockland Village and Devon Hill. By the end of the 1980s, the firm had completed in excess of 5 million square feet of commercial and residential space, as well as dozens of certified historic restorations.

During the boom years of the 1980s, I became very involved with the home-building industry, serving as the chairman of the NAHB Remodeler's Council and president of the Home Builders Association of Maryland. The firm's accomplishments were honored by three governors and numerous industry awards.

The 1990s were marred by a severe economic downturn, so I spent the last five years of the decade as a VP for the historic Maryland Jockey Club, restoring the historic racecourses at Pimlico and Laurel, as well as the OTB parlors across the state. In 1995, Governor Parris Glendening appointed me to a seat on the Maryland Historical Trust's Board of Trustees . . . a seat I still hold to this day.

Through the following years, Lone, Anthony, Matthew, and Kirsten partnered with me in the business. The culmination of my professional career was the development and construction of the world-acclaimed Ivy Hotel in Baltimore City. The endeavor took more than four years to assemble, design, and execute, and is the only hotel in Maryland ever to be admitted to the Relais & Châteaux family of the world's finest hotels.

Of course, none of this would have been possible without the steady hand of my beautiful partner-in-life, Lone Azola.

Baltimore's finest Danish import . . . Lone Azola.

When Lone first arrived in Baltimore in 1951, she couldn't speak English. Her family had hurriedly emigrated from Denmark after World War II, fearing a Russian takeover.

Her father, Odin Tidemand, and her mother, Blanca, had been particularly active in the Danish underground, so much so that Hitler had a price on Odin's head. During the Nazi occupation, the Gestapo routinely rousted them. When Odin wasn't blowing up trains, he was secretly ferrying Danish Jews to Sweden via small fishing boats in the dead of night. Blanca, a very

Odin sailing the skipjack Patty Ann on the Chesapeake

intelligent and attractive young woman, served as the decoy, distracting the troops in the front of the house, while Odin escaped out the back door. They made a great team.

Lone was the first in her family to graduate from college. During her four years at Towson State Teachers College (now Towson University), she mastered the art of teaching young people English, French, and Spanish. Her first job was teaching a sixth-grade class at Mayfield Elementary School in southwestern Virginia's coal country, where she actually had 16-year-olds in her classroom!

While we were stationed in Fairbanks, Alaska, Lone taught high school languages for four years, where she was chosen teacher of the year in 1970. In all those years, the only school closure that occurred was when a particularly heavy snow literally covered the entire structure. Huge front-end loaders from Eielson Air Force Base opened the entrances, and men hand-shoveled the roof to prevent a collapse. Typically, many of the local teachers got to school by dogsled, and it was frequently 50 degrees below zero.

Lone and Mom, Blanca

After moving back to Towson, Lone became the Towson University Alumni Association president, and toured all over the United States recruiting and visiting state associations. After three years in that position, she then moved on to further work and responsibility within the Azola family business. Lone began general administrative work at the company, and as the portfolio grew, she assumed the duties of vice president, secretary, treasurer, and, ultimately, president of Azola Building Services, LLC.

In 2006, Lone was honored as Baltimore County's "Woman of the Year" by County Executive Jim Smith, with a citation from U. S. Senator Barbara Mikulski, the Senate of Maryland, and the entire Baltimore County Council.

Now that I have retired (and, believe me, it's not going well), Lone continues to keep the books for our oldest son, Anthony, who has taken over as President of the newly restructured Azola company, Azola Building Rehab, Inc.

Anthony Azola takes the helm.

Following in my footsteps, Anthony (Tony) went to Virginia Tech and earned graduate degrees in environmental science. After graduation, he took off one year to pursue a career in professional cycling, having been chosen to train at the Olympic Training Center in Colorado.

Tony raced all over the United States and Europe as a member of a professional racing team. We remember clearly that call from Italy, right after the Tour de Abruzzi, a grueling 800-mile race through the snowcapped Italian Alps. "I have good news and bad news," he said. The bad news was that he finished in 16th position. The good news was that he was the only American to finish. He then quit racing because he refused to participate in the doping activities that appeared to be taking place in the profession.

Then, in 2006, came another call, asking if he could come home from Boston and join us in the family business. It didn't take long for Tony to get into the spirit of

Little Lucca Azola, perhaps our fourth-generation builder

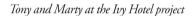

Tony and Marty at the Ivy Hotel project

rehabbing historic buildings (must be in our blood), and since then, he has held every position possible within the company, proving to be an invaluable asset to the business. He has added immeasurably to the success of every job, particularly in the areas of IT, electrical, and mechanical work, with another of his specialties involving the solving of difficult waterproofing problems.

Tony's personal best is the restoration of the historic Emerson Bromo-Seltzer Tower in downtown Baltimore. It's one of the city's most recognizable icons. Shut down due to safety concerns, he was able to devise repair methods and life-safety improvements necessary to reopen the Tower, which has become a very successful 15-story building, housing artist studios and galleries.

Presently, Tony has taken the helm as president of the Azola family business, Azola Building Rehab, Inc., and is restructuring the business to help meet the demands in today's fields of historical preservation, adaptive reuse, and interior improvement. In fact, Azola Building Rehab, Inc., was recently tapped to perform repairs to the Lincoln Memorial in Washington, DC.

As for public service, Tony has served as board chairman of Maryland's largest private statewide preservation organization, Preservation Maryland. Their advocacy has been instrumental in enhancing Maryland's preservation tax credit program, saving threatened buildings, encouraging numerous laws and ordinances, protecting historic resources, and funding non-capital programs.

Tony and his wife, Dr. Alba Azola, have one son, Lucca, and one daughter, Olivia. We should know in about 15-20 years whether or not Lucca and Olivia will become the fourth generation of Azolas to fall in love with the business of historic building preservation.

Kirsten Azola is our "go-to" person for interior design.

Kirsten Azola truly has an eye for exquisite interiors. Naturally, since our daughter grew up in the Azola family, from the earliest age everything around her, including her home, was either being remodeled, renovated, or rehabbed. So, it's not surprising that she gravitated toward the business, with an innate interest in interior design.

Prior to entering the workforce, Kirsten's love of horses was all-consuming. Her bedroom was littered with prize ribbons, trophies, and photos of her equestrian accomplishments. She kept her pony, Brooks, in the Barn at Windy Gates in the old bull's stall, until the noise from him kicking the walls became unbearable. And her Belgians were huge, but docile. Does the name Goliath paint a mental picture?

Towson University was her school of choice when that time came, with a curricular focus on design. After graduation in 2002, Kirsten began working on interior design for the company, and still does. She is our go-to person for selection of carpeting, paint colors, furnishings, and lighting.

Her work is memorialized in the finishes used at Rogers Mansion at the Maryland Zoo, Ruscombe Mansion's historic conference room and common areas, the King Syrup Plant, the Old Baltimore County Jail, the Bromo-Seltzer Tower, and others. We owe a large part of the firm's success to the visual appeal of Kirsten's choices, and we continue to work on selected projects together.

Kirsten now lives in an 11th-floor apartment in Washington, DC, where they don't allow horses. She's moved on to dogs.

The "Boys"

The Barn

Mat tearing it up at Solomon's Corner.

Matthew Azola
1977 - 2011

Matthew Azola was all about being the "hands-on" guy.

We lost Mat in the summer of 2011.

From the earliest age, all he wanted to do was to be out in the field with the guys, swinging a hammer, driving a pickup truck, and providing a fine, quality product. Mat tried college . . . four of them actually . . . but it wasn't for him.

He contributed significantly to the success of the Old Baltimore County Jail, Ruscombe Mansion, Solomon's Corner, the Barn at Windy Gates, the King Syrup Plant, and so many others.

Mat was meticulous in his work. His motto applied to every project and with every task.

"The bitterness of poor quality lingers long after the sweetness of low price is forgotten."

INDEX